10 Steps to a Digital Practice in the Cloud

New Levels of CPA Firm Workflow Efficiency

11921-356

AICPA®

John Higgins, CPA, CITP
Bryan Smith, CPA, CITP, CISA

Notice to Readers

10 Steps to a Digital Practice in the Cloud: New Levels of CPA Firm Workflow Efficiency does not represent an official position of the American Institute of Certified Public Accountants, and it is distributed with the understanding that the author and publisher are not rendering legal, accounting, or other professional services in the publication. This book is intended to be an overview of the topics discussed within, and the author has made every attempt to verify the completeness and accuracy of the information herein. However, neither the author nor publisher can guarantee the applicability of the information found herein. If legal advice or other expert assistance is required, the services of a competent professional should be sought.

3 4 5 6 7 8 9 0 PIP 1 9 8 7 6 5 4 3

ISBN: 978-1-93735-056-7

Publisher: Amy M. Plent
Senior Managing Editor: Amy Krasnyanskaya
Acquisitions Editor: Martin Censor
Developmental Editor: Suzanne Morgen
Project Manager: Charlotte Ingles
Cover Design Direction: Clay Porter

Preface

If you are picking up this book and saying to yourself, "I am too busy to read this with all of the other things I have going on in my practice," then you are precisely the person this book is targeted toward. Never before have we experienced the pace of automation of "information processing" like what we are experiencing today. That is, at least, not since our ancestors learned how to etch symbols into stone tablets to communicate.

Seriously, as CPAs, we are in the information processing business, and the indisputable fact is that information processing is being automated at an unprecedented pace. So the challenge we face is how to leverage this transformation to improve the quality, efficiency, and profitability of the services we offer our clients. In our opinion, that is the proper priority order for these three objectives. If you take care of the first two, the third is virtually guaranteed.

If you are debating whether to invest the time to read this book, ask yourself the following questions:

1. Do you want to increase the relevance of the services you provide to your clients?
2. Would you like to feel like you have made a difference in the success of your clients at the end of each day?
3. Are you concerned about keeping your team satisfied and challenged so that they stay with you and grow professionally with your firm?
4. Do you find yourself at a point in your life where you wish you had more choices on how to spend your time, for example, doing recreational activities or watching your family grow, or just spending more time relaxing in general?

We do not want to oversell the expectations of what this book has to offer, but if you answered yes to any of the previous questions, then this book will be worth the investment of your time and money.

Our primary goal is to provide accounting and tax practitioners, primarily those of you with practices that range in size from sole practitioners to mid-size firms, with an easy-to-follow roadmap for leveraging the unprecedented array of information technology solutions, or apps, that can power your practice.

As you read this book, we want you to understand that "going paperless" is not the objective. "Going digital" is. These are actually two different ways to describe a path to the same goal. So why state the distinction? The concept of "going paperless" implies giving up something we like to work with—paper. We will be the first to admit that some days, we would prefer reading a paper copy of the *Wall Street Journal* while eating breakfast. We own iPads, and we use them as a reading device in many situations; but there are times when a paper newspaper is preferred. Call us old fashioned. The real value in going paperless is in getting the data and information we need to process into a digital format so that you can strive to automate that processing as much as possible. Notwithstanding our comments about preferring to read a paper newspaper, we often get frustrated when we find ourselves processing paper documents. That means we are probably doing something that could be further automated and missing the opportunity to reduce manual efforts. We also want to be able to access it via all the different Internet-enabled devices that we use: laptops, iPads, smartphones, and whatever else comes next. Thank goodness for the "cloud" that lets us access this information at any time, from virtually anywhere! Throughout the book, we will be talking more about going digital and less about going paperless. However, at the end of the day, they are one in the same.

Before we get started, there is one important point you should keep in the back of your mind as you read this book. There is no end to the efforts you can make to automate your practice. The key is to make sure you are spending your time and money on the appropriate initiatives at the appropriate times. The best way to make this happen is to develop a plan. It does not need to be an overly complicated and detailed plan but, rather, a plan that highlights your goals and objectives for the next 12, 24, and 36 months. Do not spend a lot of time on the 36-month plan. The focus should be on the next 12 months. We will outline a process for developing this plan in chapter 13, "Developing and Implementing Your Technology Plan."

Table of Contents

Chapter 3: Infrastructure

Chapter 4: Bandwidth

Chapter 5: The CPA Technology Toolkit

Chapter 6: Scanning Solutions

Chapter 7: Document and File Management Systems

Chapter 8: Trial Balance Working Paper Software

Chapter 9: Client Portals—Gateway to the Future

Chapter 10: Workflow Software

Chapter 11: Cloud-Based Client Accounting System

Chapter 12: Security and Disaster Recovery

Chapter 13: Developing and Implementing Your Technology Plan

Chapter 14: Case Studies

Author Biographies

John H. Higgins, *CPA, CITP*

Strategic Advisor, CPA Crossings, LLC

John serves as a strategic technology advisor to CPAs in the planning and deployment of effective technology solutions and workflow automation. As a cofounder of CPA Crossings, John specializes in facilitating the development of strategic technology plans, paperless workflows, client portal solutions and a comprehensive digital practice model. He was awarded for being one of the Top 25 Thought Leaders in the accounting profession by *The CPA Practice Advisor* in 2011 and 2012. He has extensive knowledge and experience working with CPAs throughout the country and is the author of *CPA Practice Advisor's* annual Document Management Software Review, which analyzes paperless solutions for CPA practices.

Bryan L. Smith, *CPA, CITP, CISA*

Virtual CIO, CPA Crossings, LLC

Bryan serves as a virtual chief information officer (CIO) to CPA firms and professional organizations. He specializes in the planning and deployment of effective technology solutions. As a cofounder of CPA Crossings, Bryan focuses on helping firm leaders understand the issues and opportunities associated with deploying information technology to improve productivity and enhance client services and increase profitability. Bryan is the former regional director in charge of mid-market technology services for a top 10 accounting firm. He is also a nationally recognized speaker and author on technology issues affecting the CPA profession, with an emphasis on transforming to a digital practice model.

Chapter 1

The Nature of the Digital Practice Model and the Benefits to You and Your Firm

The objective of this chapter is to provide you with a foundation for understanding the overall nature of the digital practice model and how it is integral to increasing the value, quality, and profitability of your client services in the 21st century.

The Digital Practice Value Proposition

Let's start with a bird's eye view of the traditional CPA practice model pyramid in figure 1-1. The bulk of time and energy spent in your firm is most likely focused on gathering data and transforming it into meaningful information that typically results in a report of one form or another.

Figure 1-1: *The Traditional CPA Firm Practice Model*

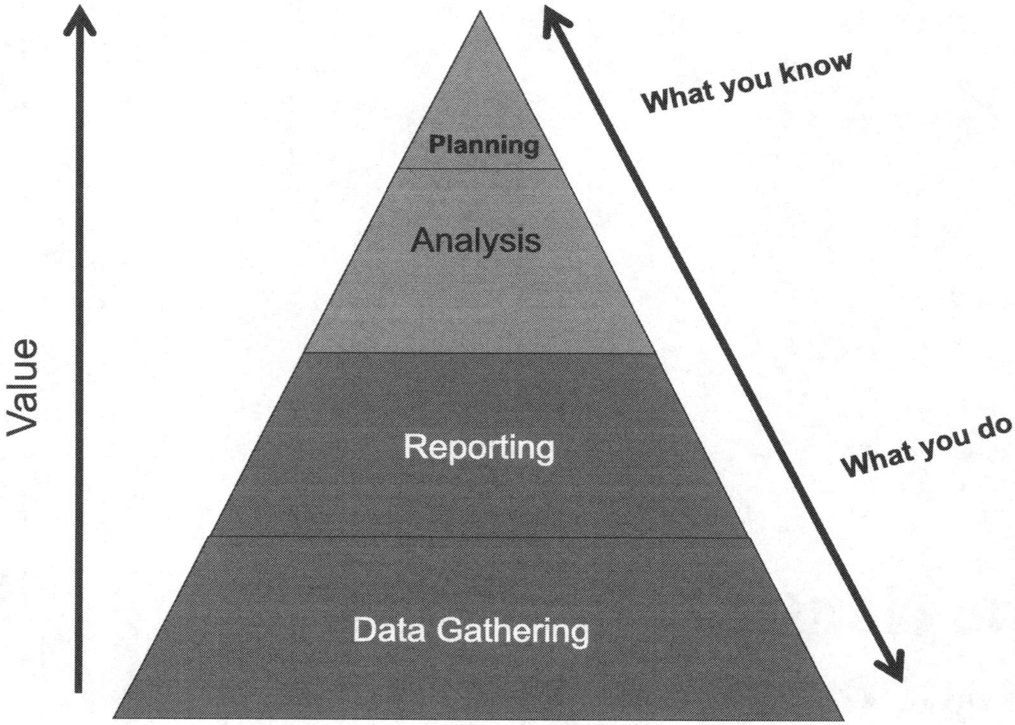

Some examples of these activities are as follows:

- Compiling transaction data into journal entries to generate financial statements that report on the financial status and performance of an organization
- Gathering individual tax data in the form of W-2s, 1099s, brokerage statements, K-1s, and so forth to prepare a 1040 tax return to measure the amount of taxes due and comply with federal and state income tax regulations
- Accumulating income and expense projection data to develop a cash flow budget to determine anticipated financing requirements
- Gathering industry information to develop a business valuation report

When you think about these individual examples, focus on where all the time is spent and where the real value is. Frankly, your clients could not care less about how much time and effort you spend in generating any of these reports other than to the extent that it affects their bill if you are still using a traditional "hours x rate fee" model. We will talk more about this in chapter 12, "Security and Disaster Recovery." The only thing your clients are really concerned with is what information the final report will provide them. In many cases, they do not know how to properly interpret the final report without your analysis and explanation. This is where the real value in your services lies because your knowledge and experience are critical to the quality and value of the services.

The key is to leverage technology as effectively as possible to automate the data processing activities that occur in the red zone, which will enable you to get that work done as efficiently and profitably as possible. Then, you can focus more of your efforts on analysis and planning services to optimize the value of your services.

We recommend that you keep the concept of this pyramid in the back of your mind every time you consider an IT initiative. Ask yourself a basic question: Will investing in this initiative result, directly or indirectly, in automating the red zone activities or increase your ability to enhance and expand your professional advisory services, or both? If you cannot answer this question in the affirmative, then you probably have an initiative that should fall toward the bottom of the list of priorities (unless it is required for regulatory purposes, privacy regulations compliance, or to mitigate risk, for example, disaster recovery planning).

One last point to mention on the pyramid is that what is happening in the accounting and tax industry is that the red zone is rapidly becoming increasingly automated at the macro market level. The challenge is to achieve this transformation at a micro level within your firm in order to remain competitive.

Key Challenges for Today's CPA Firm and Technology's Role

On any given day it may seem like your firm has an endless array of challenges to meet. We think it will help to focus here on four key challenge areas and talk about how a digital practice can help you deal with them more effectively.

Staffing

Whether the economy is up or down, the most important priority regarding your staff should be to maximize their productivity via automation. A multitude of benefits accompany this focus: greater return on investment on your personnel costs and improved employee satisfaction by continually moving them to more meaningful duties that truly leverage their professional expertise. With the proper technology solutions, a higher quality work product will result, from which everyone benefits. This is also essential from a recruitment and retention perspective. The new generation of professionals expect nothing less than a completely digital practice model and the benefits that come with it in terms of supporting a nontraditional work environment, whereby they can work when and where they want. It is not about work/life balance so much as it is about work/life integration. These, perhaps, are two sides to the same coin. But if you can foster this culture in your practice, you will move into the top percentile of "best places to work." One additional point is that the new generation is not the only one that wants the benefits of a digital practice; CPAs at all stages of their career have come to realize the benefits to them as well.

Regulation

Source: Architect of the Capitol.

We believe any objective assessment of our regulatory system would conclude that we have complicated things so much that we are putting our country and our profession at a significant competitive disadvantage in the global economy. The main point we want to make here is that technology has allowed us to automate the compliance of many regulations. Once we get the information into digital format, we have access to an abundance of software tools to process the information in a manner that is compliant with all the various regulations and standards. If you are not buying this point, download a copy of the Form 1040 and fill it out manually and keep track of all of the routine decisions you have to make that your tax preparation software currently makes for you. We believe the only way we can keep pace with the expansion of regulation is to automate the compliance with it as much as possible through technology.

Firm Succession

We suspect that many of you who choose to read this book are thinking maybe you can just ride out the technology storm for a few more years and retire to the golf course. The point we want to make here is that you have an unprecedented opportunity to systemize your business processes and client services through a digital practice model. What this means is that your client services become based more in structured and automated information delivery and less on the client knowledge that is stored inside your head. We know we are taking a risk in making this point, but if you buy into it, you will come to realize that your practice will have more value when you transition ownership. By then, you will have a well-oiled machine that is delivering your clients their financial information and services where and when they want it. Take a few minutes to ponder this objectively. Some of the most challenging transitions in firm ownership occur when the primary value is based on the partner's personal knowledge. This is because you have a natural conflict between maximizing your payout and moving toward retirement versus the value that is based on your continued involvement in the firm.

Technology

Obviously, this entire book is focused on technology, but this portion discusses the challenge of technology. It is evident that technology is changing the landscape of the accounting profession in ways that we did not even imagine just 15 or 20 years ago. Technology is going to have an even more significant impact over the next decade. Overall, the impact will be positive, but CPAs who do not take the time to develop an understanding of the direction of market forces and figure out ways to embrace the technology do so at their own peril.

Google, smartphones, iPads, cloud computing—just think about the impact that each of these recent innovations has had on the delivery of accounting and tax services. One of the difficulties of being in such a rapidly developing technological landscape is determining when a technology is ready to be embraced or if it is still too "radioactive" to risk your investment of time and money. But the greatest challenge with technology today is the abundance of choices from which you can select. It is way too easy in the current environment to make bad decisions, which is why using this book to develop a plan is so valuable. By taking the time to become informed, you can assess both the readiness and appropriateness of key technologies for your firm.

Hopefully, this review of the key challenges you face and the role that technology can play in helping you deal with them will provide further motivation to continue reading. Before you do, take a few minutes to think about this chapter and decide how valid you think these points are.

Key Trends in CPA Technology

Let's get started with a review of the four key trends in accounting and tax technology that provide the foundation for everything else that we will be discussing in this book. These trends are illustrated in figure 1-2.

Figure 1-2: *Key Trends in Accounting That Affect the Digital Practice Model*

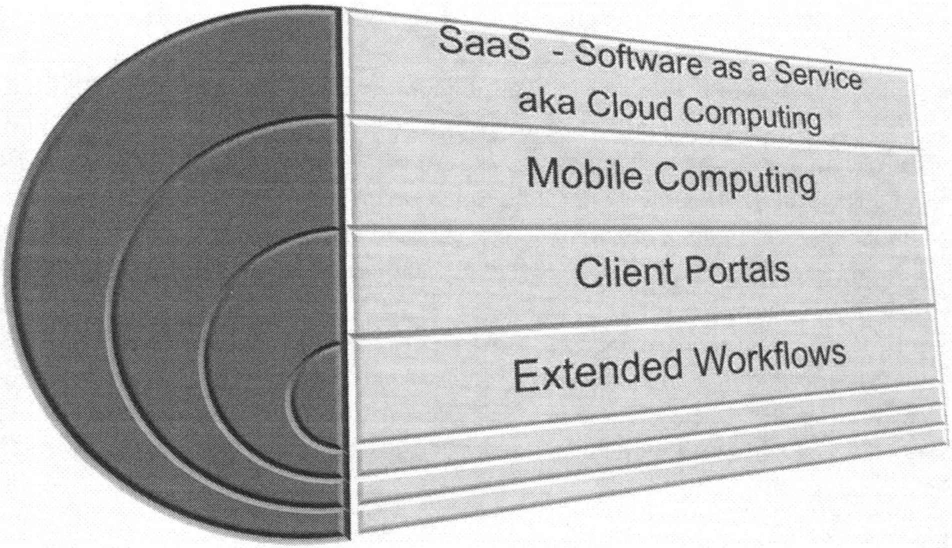

Below, we introduce and explain these four key trends. In the 30 years we have been working as CPA technology advisors, we find the environment we are currently working in to be exciting and full of opportunity. As objective CPAs, we hope that you will see how these trends affect your day-to-day practice. We also want to point out that these four trends are so interrelated that if you believe in them and fundamentally understand them, it will become relatively easy to establish the direction of your IT strategy for the coming years.

Cloud Computing aka(SaaS)

There is little question that cloud computing (also known as SaaS, or software as a service) is the most significant trend in IT today. It is a paradigm shift of unprecedented magnitude. The value proposition is undeniable. We will dive into the concept of cloud computing in chapter 3, "Infrastructure;" for now, we'll attempt a simple definition. Cloud computing is a model whereby we outsource the procurement, configuration, deployment, and management of our IT infrastructure and software applications to the specialists, which allows us to focus on the core services that we provide to our clients. It can accurately be described as IT outsourcing, but it is really so much more. Some folks do not like the concept of outsourcing. However, if you evaluate it objectively, it is a model that benefits your clients as well as your practice.

As mentioned previously, the acronym SaaS stands for software as a service, which means you are not only outsourcing your IT infrastructure, you are also transferring 100 percent of the responsibility for the performance and reliability of your software applications to the developers and vendors. The value proposition of the SaaS model is substantial. One way to consider this trend is by analogy. The evolution of the SaaS model of IT is like the arrival of the quick oil change market for automobiles. There was a time when the majority of people took responsibility for performing their own oil changes. When the oil change shops started to appear, many consumers made the shift to outsourcing this task because they could get the job done more efficiently and more effectively for a price that was easy to justify on the basis of saving your personal time for pursuit of more worthwhile activities.

Mobile Computing

For a number of years, the hype over mobile computing was questionable. The whole idea of substituting our dual monitors for a puny screen to do computer work just never seemed very appealing or practical, even though it was the "cool" thing to do. Then, along came the Apple iPad. All of a sudden, mobile computing as a paradigm shift became crystal clear to us. We could devote an entire book to this topic alone. For now, let us say that it goes hand in hand with cloud computing. The cloud takes care of our infrastructure responsibilities, and mobile computing gives us true anytime, anywhere computing. Both are key drivers of the current IT paradigm shift. The sooner you are positioned to embrace these two trends, the faster your firm's value will rise.

Client Portals

We will delve into the concept of client portals in chapter 9, "Client Portals—Gateway to the Future." Let's start by saying that we truly believe the concept of a client portal has the potential to change the CPA/client relationship for the better more than anything else in the history of the CPA profession. The client portal is the path to leveraging the value proposition of both cloud computing and mobile computing. If we were leaders of a CPA firm, one of our key strategic objectives would be to exchange the network administrator role with a portal administrator by leveraging cloud computing to eliminate the network administration responsibilities. The potential of the portal to improve the quality of your client services and the profitability of your firm is substantial. Think of it in these terms. You probably empowered your firm administrator to spearhead your selection, design, and transition to your newest office. Your client portal is more important and valuable to your clients than your office, so it deserves the allocation of the necessary resources.

Extended Workflows

With the evolution of all of these new technologies (cloud computing, mobile computing, and client portals), you have an unprecedented opportunity to redesign your business processes in order to provide your clients with better and timelier information. This can be accomplished by leveraging these various technologies to extend your workflows to include the client at strategic points along the way. It might be as simple as sending e-mail or text alerts as his or her engagement status changes or sending reminders of impending deadlines for tax filings, tax estimate payments, and other regulatory compliance. Also, the workflow extension may evolve in more substantial ways, such as facilitating a process for the client to enter his or her tax organizer data directly online through your portal. Perhaps you can automatically send a draft of the tax return or financial statement for a review by the client prior to finalizing it or possibly implementing a shared cloud-based accounting system whereby you and the client are both entering data into the same accounting database. You and the client will always be working with the same current set of data and eliminating the continuous transfer of accounting data files back and forth. This is a true shared workflow model.

As time moves forward over the next few years, we believe this will be an area in which we will experience numerous changes in the client accounting business processes. Reflect back to how your relationship with airlines has changed over the past 15 years. You can now get a continuous stream of information electronically sent to your phone, which reminds you it is time to check-in and also updates gate changes and flight status alerts. These are all automatic and very useful pieces of information created to minimize some of the frustrations associated with air travel. You always have the option to stop receiving this information if you find it becomes more of a nuisance than a benefit. We think similar workflow integrations between CPAs and their clients will have a positive impact on improving the quality of the relationship and the loyalty of the client.

As we progress through this book and take a deeper look at the specific initiatives needed to transform to a digital practice model, we will identify how these trends will affect your business process design.

Benefits of the Digital Practice Model

We already discussed how the digital practice model will help you address the key challenges that were identified at the beginning of this chapter. Let's use this opportunity to outline the benefits of transforming to a digital practice model from a more holistic perspective. The objective here is to make every effort to help you understand the value of automating your workflows.

Quality of Client Service

We cannot imagine there is a CPA who does not want to provide his or her clients with a higher quality of service. It is a fundamental success factor. Moving your practice to a digital model will improve the quality of your client services by facilitating more efficient processes. The accuracy of the information will improve because there will be fewer steps involving the manual transfer of data from point A to point B. Even the most cautious practitioners can make mistakes. In the overall picture, you will simply be spending more time analyzing and reviewing information and less time actually recording the information. Thus, your skills will be naturally applied at a higher level.

Stronger Client Relationships

The way in which humans interact with one another on an interpersonal level has changed significantly in the past few years as a result of technologies like texting, instant messaging, and e-mail. Everywhere we go, we see people with their heads down, looking at a screen of some sort. Instead of communicating with the people directly around them, they are choosing to communicate with people elsewhere via the various virtual technologies. For better or worse, that is where the world has evolved to today. So what does this have to do with a digital practice model? Once you achieve a state where you can deliver and exchange information with your clients electronically, you can work toward making your firm the place they visit online on a regular basis to access their business and personal financial center. You want to keep pushing the envelope with innovative ways to reach out to your clients in a virtual world. It may be through a web conferencing session to walk them through the process of filling out the tax organizer or providing them access to their entire collection of online financial information in a single place (your portal). Perhaps it is sending them important alerts via e-mail or text to expand the level of communication you have with them. The more you leverage the digital practice model to develop these communication links to your clients, the stronger your relationships will be because you will be in their virtual space much more than you were ever in their personal space.

Do More With Less Effort

Refer back to the practice paradigm pyramid and contemplate the red zone. Every time you are successful in implementing a technology initiative that automates a piece of your business processes, you are making a deposit in the time savings account. If technology exists that can automate a task, then that is one more task you probably should not be doing manually. The time you save through automation can be reallocated to increase the volume of your services without increasing personnel resources. Or you can refocus more of your efforts on the higher value analysis and advisory services, or you can simply take more time back for your personal life. The bottom line is that if technology can do it for you cost effectively, why not make that choice?

Enhance the Overall Value of Your Firm

The accumulation of all the benefits described in this chapter will result in three very strategic benefits to your firm: increased profitability, increased value, and stronger client relationships. This will provide you with greater resources to invest back into your staff, your office, your technology, your service offerings, and yourself. This will also result in pushing up the valuation of your practice when it comes time to transition the ownership.

Chapter 2

The 10 Steps to a Digital Practice

This chapter introduces what we believe are the 10 key steps to becoming a truly digital practice and gaining all the benefits of this model. We put them in the order we think is most practical because they will need to be completed over an extended period of time. However, your situation is unique to your practice and, therefore, you may have different priorities. This is another reason why it is important to have a plan.

Strategic View of IT Model

When we discuss the topic of IT or information systems, we are talking about a pretty broad scope of territory. Today, there are so many different facets to an information system that it requires further clarification about what aspect is being addressed at any given point in time.

Before we introduce the 10 key steps to a digital practice, we think it is important to define the basic elements and hierarchy of an IT system. In order to provide a framework for our discussion of the steps that you need to take to go digital, figure 2-1 illustrates a strategic view of the IT model, with the objectives for each component in parentheses. Each component plays an important role and requires a different approach to properly address it. Also, every firm is in a different place in terms of where the current priorities should be

Figure 2-1: *Strategic Digital Firm Framework Model*

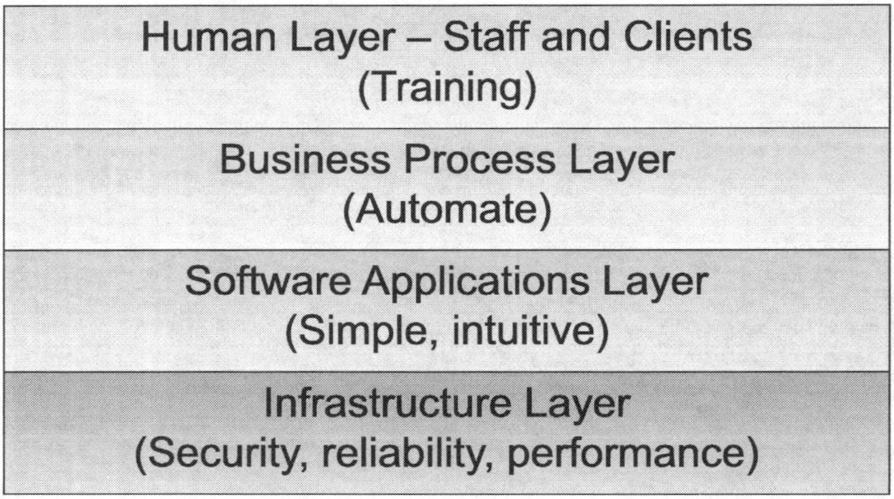

assigned. Where you focus your time and money first maybe the biggest challenge you face with your IT system.

Infrastructure

The infrastructure can be defined broadly or narrowly. For purposes of our discussion, we will define *infrastructure* as your file servers, shared storage devices, network operating systems, secondary storage devices, power backup, routers, and internal or external data communications network. It is the backbone of your system, the "plumbing" that allows the information and data to flow to and from your personal computers, laptops, and mobile devices.

In this day and age, it is not uncommon to have multiple servers in your infrastructure, which can consist of file servers, the Exchange server, the Citrix server, SQL servers, Internet servers, and so forth. Traditionally, each server was a physical computer. However, with the innovation of virtualization, you can now consolidate these servers into one single, physical server. We will discuss the topic of infrastructure in chapter 3, "Infrastructure." The main point to get across now is that cloud computing has provided accounting firms with a reliable, secure, and cost-effective solution for addressing your infrastructure needs.

Software Applications

The software applications layer consists of various applications that help you automate your business processes, such as tax, research, audit working papers, practice management, client accounting, document management, portal, Microsoft Office, and so forth. It is the software that puts your infrastructure to work. The good news is that an abundance of quality software applications are currently available from a variety of quality vendors to automate your practice. The challenge is figuring out which solution is best suited for each of your business processes. Again, cloud computing has really advanced in the supply of quality software solutions because they can be very easily deployed in the software as a service (SaaS) model. The best part about the SaaS model is that the infrastructure is provided by the vendor as a by-product. Therefore, with cloud computing, you can effectively address the two foundational layers through an outsourced model.

Business Processes

The business process layer is ultimately the point at which you realize the benefits of all the time and money invested in your IT systems. Think back to the practice pyramid diagram. At the end of the day, it is all about automating your processes as much as possible to increase productivity and the value of your time. This is where the real value of cloud computing is realized because we are able to minimize the effort required to deploy the technology. We are now able to place a much greater emphasis on the application of technology. Ideally, you should be directing the bulk of your attention on automating your workflows. Unlike the 1980s and '90s, when IT was disproportionately focused on getting the infrastructure deployed and working with the software, cloud computing has addressed that role for us in large measure. The key to putting your firm at a strategic competitive advantage is by continually working to improve your processes through automation.

Staff and Clients

The human layer of the IT model is arguably the most important and addresses the interaction between the staff and the technology you have deployed to execute your business processes. The user experience can spell the difference between success and failure in your IT initiatives. The key at this layer is training. Whenever we perform an assessment of a firm's IT model, training inevitably ends up as one of the top three issues a firm is having based on staff survey. The typical problem with training is that there is always an over emphasis on how to operate the software (that is, how do I create an Excel spreadsheet, how do I convert documents to PDF format, how do I format a financial statement, and so forth). Although that level of training is important, what often gets overlooked is training on how to apply the technology in terms of integrating it into a specific process. For example, at what point in the tax preparation process do we publish the return to PDF format? Additionally, what security restrictions will we put on it, how will we communicate the password key to the client, and what is our retention policy for the document?

If you want to know how to change this training culture in your firm, discontinue software training and, instead, approach all your training as business process training. Focus on walking through all the steps to complete a particular process, for example, tax return preparation. Inevitably, this training will have to incorporate the software application component in order to train your staff to get the tasks completed. The very nature of this approach to training will incorporate only those software features that are relevant and how to apply them.

Another very important point to understand about the people layer is that "users" now include clients and other third parties, for example, loan officers. With the evolution of cloud computing and client portals, we are now extending access to our IT systems to people outside of our organizations. When you step back and consider this, it is a huge shift in the information services paradigm. We believe the accounting industry is poised to leverage technology through a transition similar to what banks and airlines have done over the last 10–15 years. Just stop and think about how the nature of the way you interact with these service providers has shifted. Their workflows have been extended to you, as the customer, through their IT systems. You are doing much of the work they used to do for you, such as booking a reservation and transferring money between accounts. You are probably a lot more satisfied with the process because you are more in control of the transaction and can get what you need at any time, from virtually anywhere, with cloud computing and mobile computing solutions.

In reality, what has happened in those industries is that their red zone has been automated. The customer service personnel were essentially entering the information you provided into their system or relaying to you information that they pulled out of the system. So now they just link the customer directly to the IT system and eliminate the redundancy of the efforts their staff fulfilled previously. For better or worse, this type of displacement is happening in nearly every service industry to one degree or another. You just have to ask yourself whether you feel the way you interact with the banks and airlines has improved or deteriorated. Keep in mind we are only talking about the business process here, so be objective and do not include the pricing model changes, such as increased bank charges and luggage fees. That is a whole different issue and another lesson to be learned.

The main point here is that you now have the tools available to significantly enhance the quality and timeliness of your client interactions with your firm by giving them greater access to a broader array of information and services through your portal. To summarize, keep the IT model in the back of your mind as you assess the state of your business processes and the information system that supports them. It should help you to do a better job of prioritizing where to make your investments and expend your time.

The 10 Steps

Now that you have an overview of the IT model, we are ready to delve into the 10 steps to a digital practice. We will introduce these 10 initiatives here and then explore each of them in the subsequent chapters. The main steps we have identified are substantial and include many subordinate steps, so try not to get hung up on the number but, rather, focus on the substance. The 10 steps are illustrated in the following graphic:

As you can see, the technology plan is at the center of all the initiatives. Because there are so many things to do and so many ways to do them, you have to develop the plan. We will provide some useful guidance on how to go about this process in the last chapter.

Figure 2-2: *The 10 Step Technology Plan*

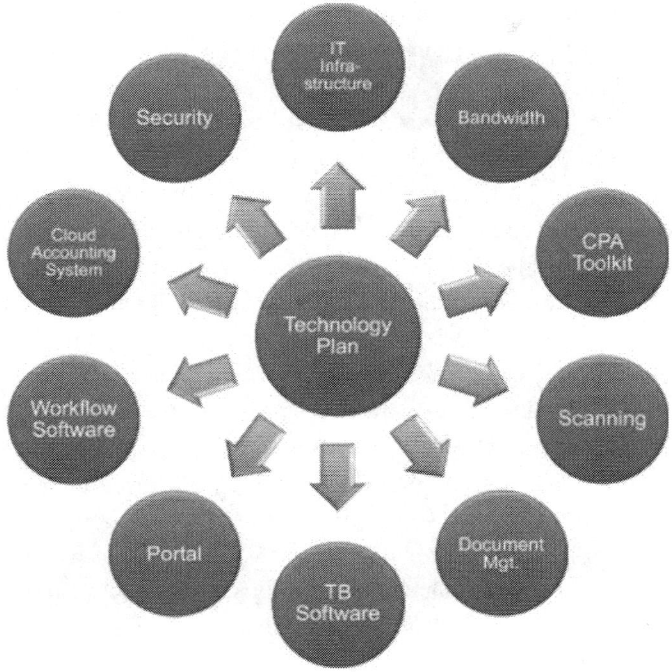

10 Steps to a Digital Practice Model

1. **Infrastructure.** As discussed previously, this is the foundation for your IT system. We will explore the alternative approaches to addressing your IT infrastructure by leveraging the cloud, including managed services, data center hosting, and SaaS.
2. **Bandwidth.** The more we become dependent on the Internet, the more we rely on the data communications services that allow us to drive on the information superhighway. In this chapter, we will delve into the concepts and terminology that you need to be familiar with to ensure that you implement the optimal broadband solution(s) for your practice, which will include both wired and wireless.
3. **CPA technology toolkit.** This is all about the collection of hardware and software products that you need to outfit your individual staff members. This includes desktops and laptops, tablets, smartphones, Microsoft Office, Adobe Acrobat, and more. We will provide a detailed blueprint that will put you in a position to achieve maximum productivity by leveraging the most cost-effective solutions.
4. **Scanning solutions.** Some practices have more paper to deal with than others, but we all have to deploy a solution to convert the paper documents into electronic images in our workflows as early in the process as possible in order to leverage the full benefits of going paperless.

5. **Document Management Systems (DMS).** This initiative is not easy and not necessarily cheap, but it is an essential component to developing the optimal digital practice model. We will explain the essence of DMS and what you need to consider when deploying a solution.
6. **Trial balance (TB) working paper software.** Many of you may have already implemented this software in your practice. It is essentially a hybrid of the DMS and workflow software designed specifically for trial balance based engagements, such as business tax returns, audits, reviews, and compilations. The value of this application is in direct relation to the volume of TB engagements you perform.
7. **Client portals.** You get to the full potential of the digital practice model by transforming your website into a personalized, private, and secure financial center for your clients. If approached with the proper mindset, the client portal can do more to change the profitability of your practice than any of the other initiatives presented.
8. **Workflow software.** The first objective with this initiative is to develop an understanding of what it is all about. Essentially, workflow software is the tool that facilitates the movement of your engagements through their business processes in a paperless world. Think about how you have traditionally managed engagements with red rope folders, routing sheets, checklists, review notes, and so forth. A good workflow application will automate all of that and provide a lot more in terms of management reporting.
9. **Cloud-based accounting systems.** This is a solution that is poised to significantly improve the business process for delivering client accounting services via the cloud. The market is more than ready to move beyond the traditional model of swapping accounting system data files back and forth between the client and the CPA. By leveraging the cloud, you can provide a much higher quality of service whereby you are analyzing and adjusting your client's financial data in real time.
10. **Security and disaster recovery.** This initiative is analogous to going to the dentist's office. We do not typically want to deal with the whole experience. However, we know it is a necessary part of our personal health care and hygiene, and we typically feel much better when we have completed the process. So it goes with IT security and disaster recovery planning. If you take the time to address these two key initiatives, you will have a heightened level of confidence in your system and the protection of your client's data and privacy. The good news is that with cloud computing, the ability to secure and protect your information becomes a lot easier via the data center model.

Chapter 3

Infrastructure

As we depicted in figure 2-1 in chapter 2, "The 10 Steps to a Digital Practice," infrastructure is the foundation for your entire information system. Therefore, it requires nothing less than a complete focus on reliability, performance, and security. The good news is that through the use of secure data centers and cloud computing, it is much easier and more cost effective to develop a world class IT infrastructure for even the smallest accounting and tax practice.

Infrastructure Defined

If you ask 10 different IT professionals to define *infrastructure*, you are likely to get 10 different answers. However, they will all agree on the fundamental components. To help simplify the definition, table 3-1 identifies the components of infrastructure. We have put each item into one of two categories: server-based infrastructure and peripheral. The reason for doing this is that as we discuss leveraging the cloud computing model, it is the server-based infrastructure that is moved to the data center, and some of the peripheral components remain on premise. Note that some items fall into both categories.

Table 3-1: *IT Infrastructure Components*

Infrastructure Components	Server-Based	Peripheral
File server(s)	X	
Network operating system	X	
Storage drives	X	
Firewall hardware and software	X	X
Routers	X	X
Switches	X	X
Data back-up devices	X	
Back-up power system	X	
Data communications network hardware	X	X
Data communication services	X	X
Printers		X
Scanners		X
PCs/laptops/smartphones/tablets		X

You have four basic alternative approaches to addressing your server-based infrastructure today. We have defined each of these and pointed out the pros and cons of each option in the following list:

1. **Traditional.** On-premise server infrastructure managed by internal staff.
2. **Managed service.** On-premise server infrastructure managed by external service provider via the cloud, or managed service.
3. **Hosting.** Data center hosting of server infrastructure managed by the service provider and accessed by your personnel via the cloud.
4. **Software as a service (SaaS).** Data center hosting of server infrastructure provided by software vendor as a by-product of delivering the application via the cloud, or SaaS.

With the exception of option one, all the other options deploy the cloud computing model in one form or another, which is why so many people get confused about the concept. Just remember that the Internet is the cloud, and the cloud is the Internet. So when the term *cloud computing* is thrown around, all it really means is that the information or service is delivered via the Internet's world wide data communications network. Notwithstanding this explanation of the cloud, when people refer to cloud computing today, they are overwhelmingly referring to the SaaS model. This is the fastest growing segment of the accounting and tax technology marketplace. Now let's analyze these four options in detail.

Traditional On-Premise Model

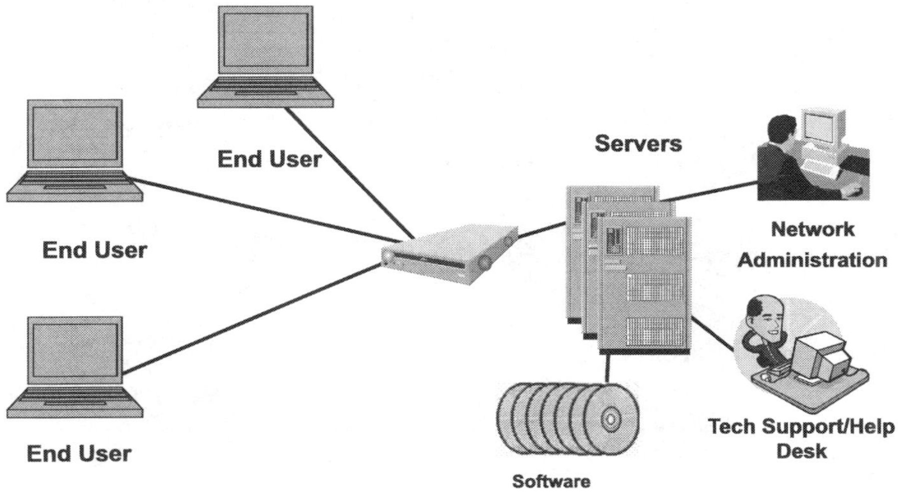

We refer to this as the *traditional* model because it is has been the de facto infrastructure model in place in most business organizations for the past 30 years, since the advent of the personal computer. We do not need to spend a lot of time discussing this model because you are most likely all too familiar with it already.

The traditional model is based on deploying your entire infrastructure internally, or *on premise*, as it is referred to today. Your servers, routers, switches, peripherals, virtually all the infrastructure components listed in the preceding figure are located on-site in your office. Sometimes, they are in a well-controlled server room environment, and sometimes they are set up as a makeshift computer room in a closet or open cubicle.

The biggest challenge with this model consists of employing a network administrator with the requisite skill set to configure, deploy, and manage your infrastructure and protect the physical security of the equipment and the programs and data that are stored on it. This model has become increasingly demanding for most accounting firms because the number and complexity of the servers that need to be deployed have expanded substantially over the years. You have your primary file server for storing your software applications and shared data. You probably have a SQL server for those applications that require an SQL database. This technology alone requires a more advanced IT skill set to deploy and manage. You probably have a Microsoft Exchange server that extends your user's Outlook applications to an enterprise solution to manage your e-mail communications and share access to calendars and common folders for information such as the enterprise's contact database. You may have an Internet server to manage your Internet communications and possibly redundant servers to provide a measure of disaster recovery protection. The mere fact that you have multiple servers makes for a complex infrastructure to maintain. Fortunately, current server technology has evolved to a point in which these physical servers can be consolidated into a single server using "virtualization" technology, but this takes another advanced skill set to deploy and manage.

So you can understand the challenge of finding and retaining the appropriately qualified staff to handle all these complexities, let alone the capital investment that is required to procure, deploy, and manage this infrastructure. It is typical to retain some level of external support to supplement the skills and abilities of your internal staff, but this comes at an additional expense. Of the four infrastructure models discussed here, the traditional model is the only one that is clearly on a negative growth path as a result of the value proposition of the rapidly emerging cloud-based solutions.

Managed Service Model

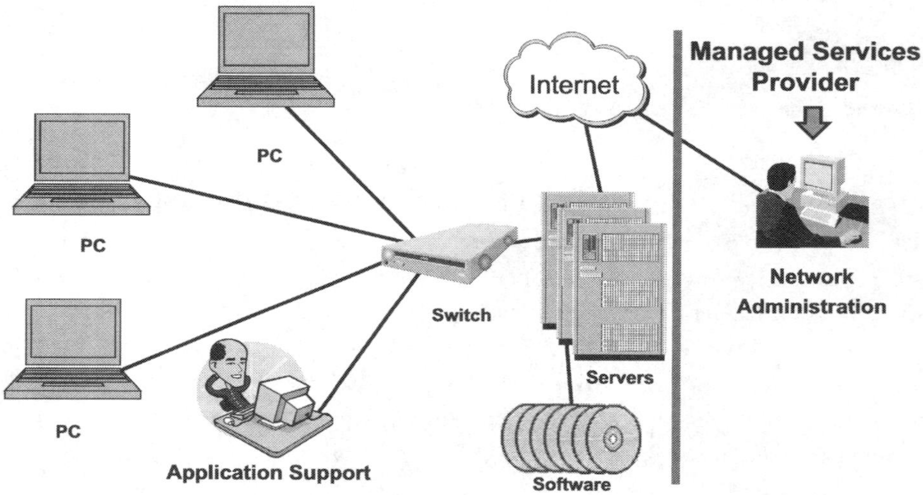

This is essentially an extension of the traditional model that leverages the cloud by utilizing the services of a dedicated external IT support organization via cloud computing. These service providers can provide virtually all your IT support requirements from their remote service center. The benefit of this is a shared services model that enables the service provider to employ a team of skilled specialists to handle all the different levels of support required. Also, through economies of scale, they can provide the service on a cost-effective basis. If you have 20 separate accounting practices, each with its own internal IT staff, there is inevitably going to be either idle capacity or a misallocation of technical resources. If all 20 firms share the services of a single managed service provider, the opportunity to establish a more effective allocation of technical resources is virtually assured.

As a point of clarification, the managed service model means that you continue to procure your own infrastructure and deploy it internally, on premise. So you still have the challenge of making the capital investments necessary to continue upgrading your information system to optimize performance and reliability. You also retain the responsibility of procuring and managing your applications software in most situations.

It is not at all uncommon to deploy a mixed model of a traditional infrastructure with some level of internal IT staff working in cooperation with the personnel from the managed service provider. So it is essentially a hybrid model. Having the service provider "team" ready and able to support your internal staff removes a major source of stress in managing your IT system.

Managed Service Value Proposition

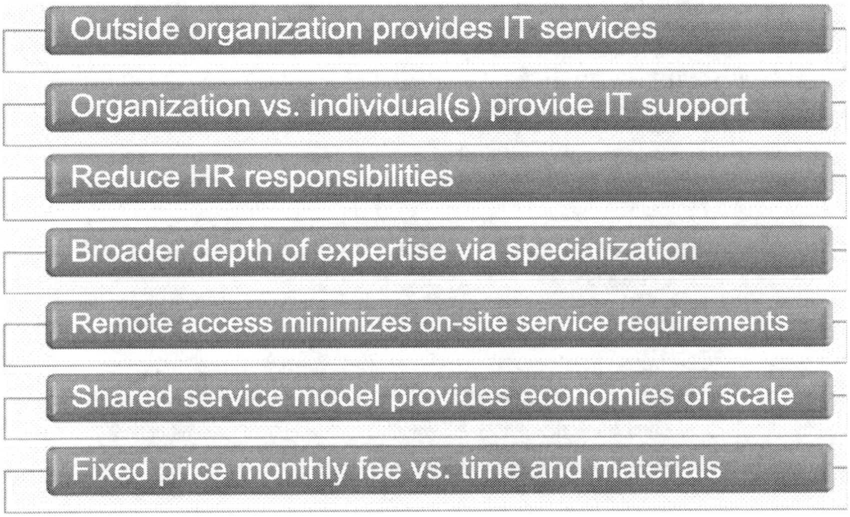

Data Center Hosting Model

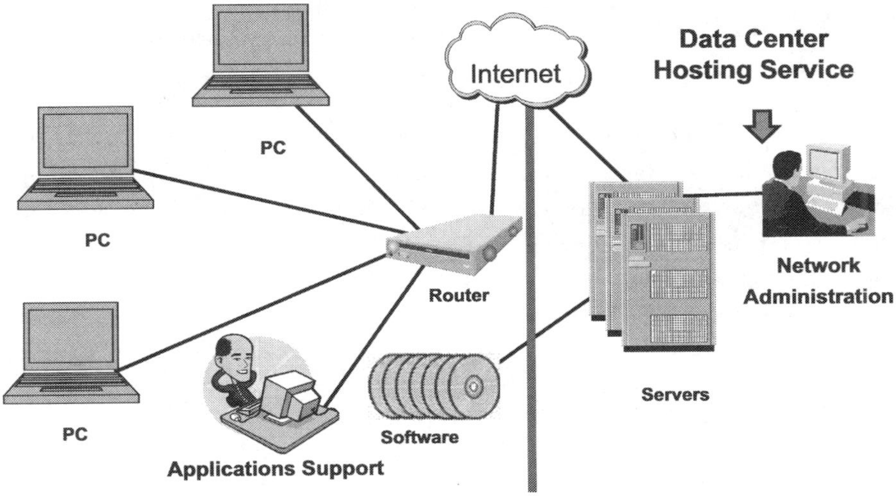

The primary characteristic of this model is that you move your entire physical server infrastructure off-site to a secure data center that is managed by the service provider. There are different flavors of the hosting model. In some cases, you are required to provide your own server infrastructure equipment and deploy it in a secure cage (literally) at the data center, whereby all customers share access to the supporting infrastructure, including cabling, data communications, physical security measures, disaster recovery protection, and so forth. Some hosting companies provide a more comprehensive service that includes purchasing your server equipment directly from them, so that they can provide a more controlled environment to enhance the overall reliability of your infrastructure by utilizing equipment that their staff has experience with. The cloud comes into play in this model because now your personnel are accessing your remotely hosted server infrastructure via the Internet.

Data Center Hosting Value Proposition

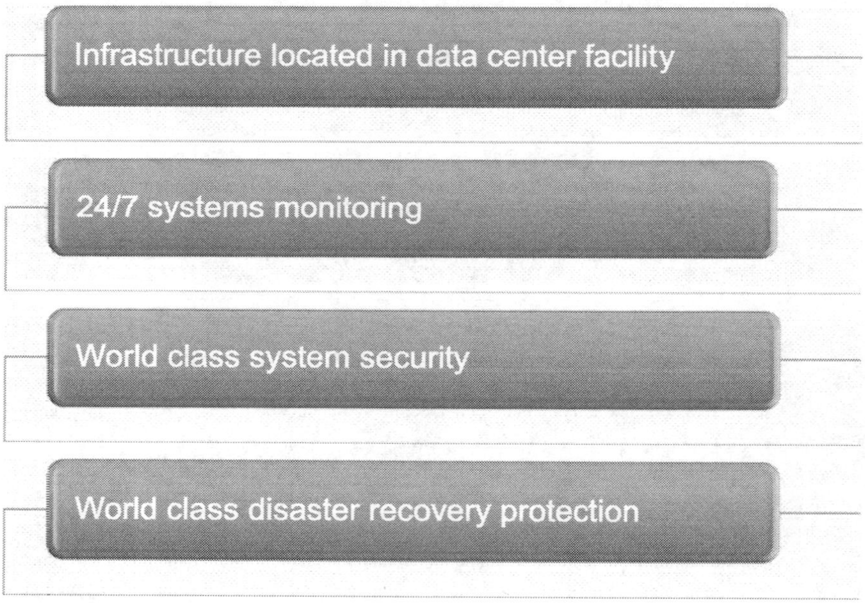

In summary, the three models discussed thus far all have common characteristics, including investing in your infrastructure equipment and maintaining ultimate responsibility for the infrastructure and software applications. The managed service and hosting models provide for a certain level of outsourcing of your IT systems management, whereas the traditional model is all done in-house.

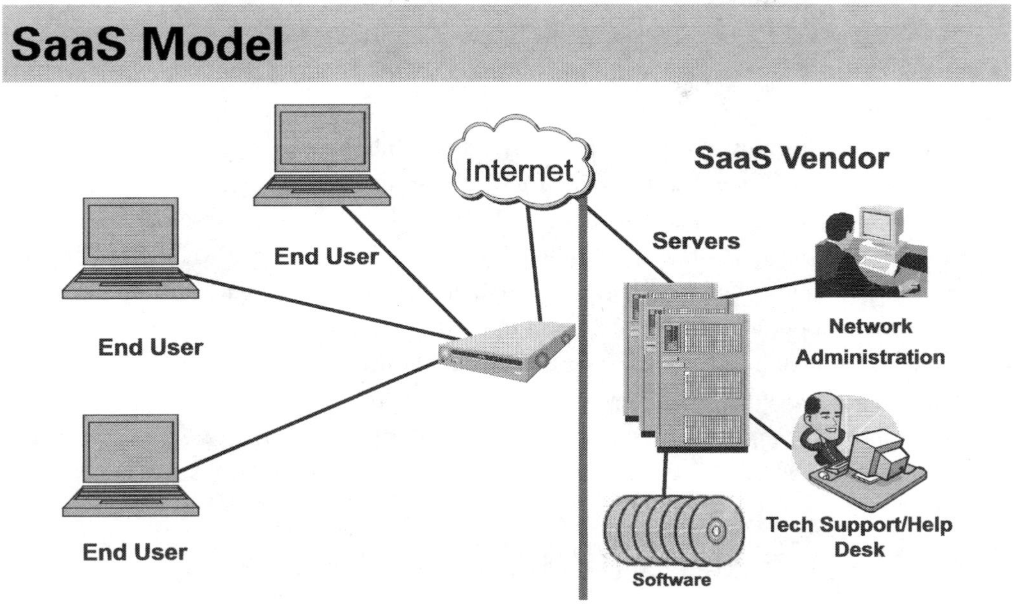

When you hear the term *cloud computing* these days, it is the SaaS model that is typically being referenced. What distinguishes the SaaS model from all the other forms of cloud computing is that the focus is on the software application, rather than the infrastructure. In fact, the infrastructure is provided simply as a by-product of the application. That is the essence of where the term originated. You get everything required to run the application through your Internet browser, which makes the deployment of the application exponentially simpler than the traditional on-premise model because you do not have to worry about investing in or deploying the required infrastructure. It is delivered as part of the service.

The bottom line on the SaaS model is that it has been the fastest growing segment of the accounting and tax technology market in recent years, due primarily to the value proposition of this "turnkey" solution model.

SaaS Value Proposition

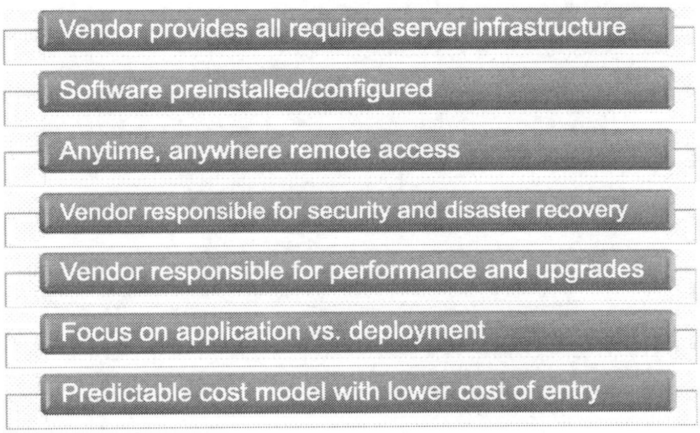

We have covered infrastructure as the first step because your strategy here has widespread implications on your entire information system model. Despite the fact that we have defined each model independently, the reality is that most firms will deploy a hybrid. The primary metric for evaluating your options is the suitability of the applications themselves. You must continually focus on deploying the applications that will optimize your ability to automate your processes. What is taking place in the marketplace today is that virtually all new software innovation is being delivered through the cloud via the SaaS model. In our opinion, it seems quite obvious that this is a paradigm shift that will eventually result in virtually all software applications being delivered in the SaaS model. The more relevant question is what is the optimal timing to move a particular application from on premise to the cloud? The answer will be different for every firm based on the current applications deployed, expansion into new applications, the state of your current IT infrastructure, and your firm's strategy for obtaining your IT support services.

Security in the Cloud

One of the primary impediments to the adoption of cloud computing in the market place 5–10 years ago was concern about the security of information transmitted via the Internet and stored on remote Web-accessible servers. Ironically, the situation has reversed as a result of greater education and awareness of security measures that can be implemented to protect your information in the cloud. We have provided a detailed discussion of this in chapter 12, "Security and Disaster Recovery," which focuses on security. We have also included links in appendix C, "Resource Center," to a sample of the security specifications for a first class data center, as well as a link to detailed information on the AICPA's new Service Organization Controls reports (formerly known as a SAS No. 70 reports). We encourage you to review this information to increase your understanding and confidence in the depth of security provided with cloud computing.

Chapter 4

Bandwidth

We placed this as the second step simply because it is a natural extension of your infrastructure strategy. As mentioned in the previous chapter, the IT paradigm is rapidly transitioning to an outsourced model through managed services, data center hosting, software as a service, or a combination. All these new models require high speed data transfer via the Internet, so this will become one of the core components of your IT model going forward. In this chapter, we will explain key concepts related to data communications and provide practical guidance for procuring the best solution(s) for your firm.

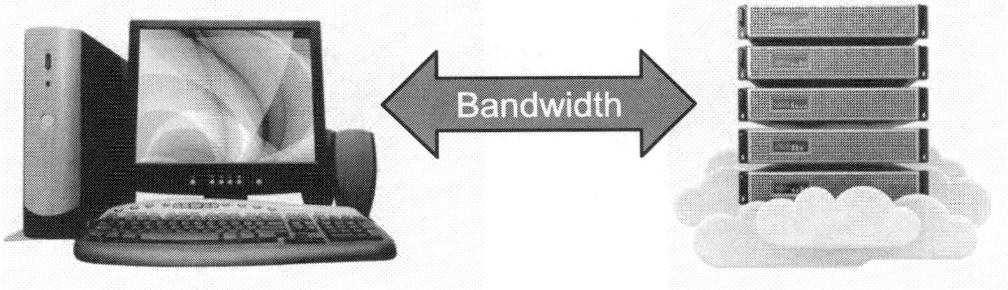

Bandwidth Defined

Bandwidth, in this context, refers to the capacity to transfer digital data between two devices. More accurately, it measures the speed and capacity of the data communication service that you deploy to transfer information between two devices. In the world of cloud computing, we use bandwidth to transfer data to and from cloud-based servers to our local devices, including desktops, laptops, tablets, smartphones, and so forth.

The more we rely on the cloud, the more we rely on having secure, reliable, and fast bandwidth. It is the virtual lifeline of cloud-based computing. The bottom line is that you cannot have too much bandwidth in this day and age, except for the fact that you do not want to pay for more than you need. The good news is that if you outsource your entire server infrastructure via cloud computing, you have much less technology to deal with on the premises. However, data communication services, and the bandwidth provided, has become one of the most important aspects of your IT model. Therefore, our focus in this chapter is on explaining the different types of bandwidth available, where to procure it, and how to determine your firm's requirements.

Measuring Bandwidth

We measure bandwidth as the amount of data that can be carried from one point to another over a given time period (usually a second). The most common metric used is bits per second (bps). Back in the 1980s, bandwidth speeds were typically measured in the kilobits per second (Kbps) (1,204 bits) range. Today, most bandwidth is measured in megabits per second (Mbps), and we have now moved into the era of gigabits per second (Gbps). To give you just one simple example of how much a megabit translates into in terms of typical file sizes, a 75-page PDF file containing scanned 1040 source documents weighed in at approximately 18,150 kilobytes, or 1.8 mbs. Therefore, on a typical cable based service, this file would take a second or 2 to download.

Bandwidth Requirements

It is really about much more than just bandwidth. You have to deploy a complete data communications infrastructure to access the bandwidth to communicate between devices (outlined in figure 4-1). Let's take a look at the pieces of the puzzle that are required.

Figure 4-1: *Data Communication Model*

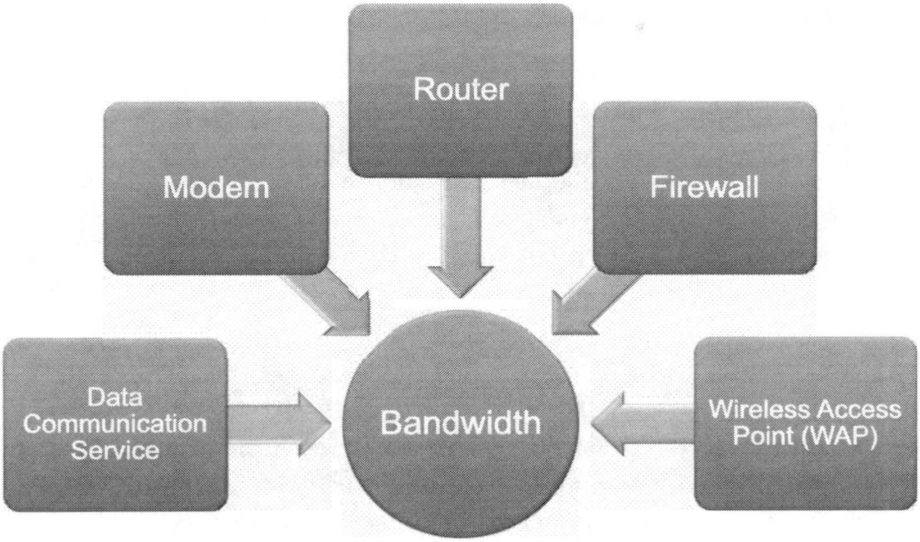

Data Communication Service

This is what actually transmits your data across the network. You purchase it from a service provider, such as the telephone company, cable company, or cellular service provider. We will talk more about the options later.

Modem

If you are using a wired data communications service, then you will need a modem device. Without getting too technical, this device converts the data from packets that are distributed through the data communications network into packets that get distributed to your internal network devices. The data travels between IP addresses, which are assigned to every device on the network. This is similar to the way postal addresses are used to distribute mail throughout the world. The bottom line is that the modem is the link between the external data network and your internal network. Typically, the modem will be provided by the Internet service provider, which is the preferred option because then they are responsible for compatibility and configuration. If not, you can buy one at a local electronics store.

Router

This device manages the distribution of the data packets that pass through the modem to your internal network. This distribution is based on the IP addresses described previously. Think of the router as the mailman delivering letters to the proper addresses. Some devices combine the functions of the modem and router into a single unit.

Wireless Access Point

A wireless access point (WAP) is an optional component if you want to connect to your broadband service wirelessly. Quite often, the data communications service provider's modem or router will have the WAP built in. Otherwise, you will need to buy a WAP unit and connect it to your router. The WAP will extend and distribute your broadband wirelessly to your wireless-enabled devices (desktops, laptops, printers, tablets, smartphones, and so forth).

Firewall

As the name implies, this component is designed to provide a virtual security gate that manages what data gets into your network via your data communications service, as well as what data gets sent out. The concept of a firewall is as follows: It is a combination of hardware and software that is inserted in the broadband chain between your modem and your router. Often, it is the same physical device. The firewall is programmable and requires a fairly deep level of knowledge of IT security concepts.

Wired Versus Wireless

There is good news and bad news. The good news is that you have a multitude of options for procuring bandwidth for your firm. The bad news is that with so many options to choose from, it can get overwhelming to try and determine the optimal solution. We will try and explain the alternative bandwidth options available, so that you can become an educated buyer.

We have been using the term *bandwidth* extensively up to this point, but to be technically more precise, what we are really talking about is broadband. The term *broadband* is generally used to describe a multichannel telecommunication service that can transfer digital data of all types at a relatively high rate of speed. The capacity of the broadband service is commonly measured in terms of bandwidth.

Broadband can be categorized into two primary groups: wired and wireless. They are not mutually exclusive. Wireless broadband is always an extension of wired broadband service somewhere along the way. Most of the time, the wired broadband is coming directly into your office or home, and you connect a wireless router or access point to it in order to distribute the bandwidth wirelessly for the last leg of the journey. There are exceptions of course. If you use satellite or cellular broadband, then the bandwidth will be delivered wirelessly from a much further distance, that is, a cellular tower. Frankly, you do not really need to worry about some of those details. However, we do want to provide a basic description of the major broadband alternatives so that you will understand the differences when select the optimal service for your firm.

Wired Service Options

DSL (Digital Subscriber Line)

Widely known as asymmetric DSL to data providers, DSL is provided over standard, copper wire telephone lines but requires a DSL filter if it will be used simultaneously with telephone service. Without the filter, the data connection will receive interference from the telephone service and become unreliable. DSL is the most commonly used data connection because it travels over copper wire, which is common in most homes and businesses throughout the United States as the core landline telephone service. The data speed is dependent on the line conditions, the specific DSL technology service available in that area, and the service level implementation. Download speeds are faster than upload speeds on a DSL. However, a symmetric DSL (SDSL) may be available, which has the same download and upload speeds. Speeds range from 256 KB per second to 40 MB per second, which is obviously a wide range to choose from when procuring your broadband service. Installation of a DSL should be via a dedicated DSL line or outlet. This will prevent the DSL signal from being transmitted across the entire phone system, an effect called *attenuation*. So the key things to look for with DSL include upload and download speed, whether a filter is provided, and whether the line is dedicated. One of the best ways to evaluate this is to check if others in your building have the DSL service you are looking to procure and ask them to run a speed test for you so you can see the results yourself.

Tier 1–5 (T1, T2, T3, T4, and T5)

The T-Carrier system was introduced in the early 1960s. Its data transfer speed is rated at a fixed speed of 1.544 Mbps download and upload. A T2 line is a bundle of 4 T1 lines for a speed of 6,312 Mbps. A T3 line is a bundle of 28 T1 lines that provide a speed of 44.736 Mbps. T-carrier lines are provided by local Bell operating companies, such as AT&T, Verizon, and Qwest, or competitive local exchange carriers, such as Covad, tw telecom, Windstream, and XO Communications.

Cable

Cable Internet access uses the cable television infrastructure and is typically connected via coaxial or fiber optic cable. Data speeds can be as high as 400 Mbps for download and 20 Mbps for upload but are typically in the 2 MB–12 MB range. Cable Internet service initially started as a residential service but is rapidly expanding into commercial service. Cable service shares bandwidth with all users on a common core network. This allows them to leverage the available bandwidth while keeping the cost reasonable. The downside is that if many or all users are on the core network at one time, there could be a noticeable decrease in performance. This is often seen in neighborhoods when all the children and parents return home from school and work and before they go to bed. You can typically purchase different classes of service from the cable company, so evaluate the options. As with DSL service, if you are in a shared office building, visit one of the other tenants using the cable service and ask them to do a speed test for you.

Wireless Service Options

Wi-Fi (Wireless Fidelity)

The beauty of Wi-Fi is that your device is untethered. You do not have to run a myriad of cables through your office or be constrained by using your device only where you can "plug-in." Wi-Fi is often referred to as a *hotspot* and is found in various public and private establishments, such as coffee shops, restaurants, hotels, airports, airplanes, and libraries. Some Wi-Fi hotspots are free, whereas others charge by the minute, hour, day, or month. They may also limit the amount of download and upload traffic (data) a user transfers, so be sure to check the fine print. Some communities are attempting to provide community-wide Wi-Fi access as a public service; however, there is an important caveat. Most of these public and private Wi-Fi hotspots do not implement encrypting technology, which means data is transmitted in plain text and may be intercepted and seen by others on the network. Be careful about transmitting personal information, for example, tax returns via Wi-Fi networks. You can determine if a Wi-Fi connection is using encryption security if it requires a login password. The speed of a Wi-Fi network can vary substantially based on a number of factors. The bottom line is that you should expect a typical Wi-Fi connection to operate in the 10–25 Mbps range. The next generation of Wi-Fi is projected to reach speeds of up to 1 Gbps (1,000 Mbps), which should have an extremely positive impact on the use of cloud-based applications.

Cellular (3G, 4G)

Cellular wireless service is often referred to as *mobile broadband* and is provided by the cellular phone companies. Similar to DSL and cable Internet access, mobile broadband uses an existing network to provide data communications and Internet access. Various network strategies and technologies are dependent on the particular cellular company's infrastructure. In the United States, there are two basic types of 3G services: CDMA2000/EVDO (Verizon, Sprint, Alltel, Cricket, MetroPCS, US Cellular) and UMTS/HSPA (AT&T, T-Mobile.) There are various versions of these 3G technologies, and the speeds range from 384 Kbps to 42 Mbps for download and 384 Kbps to 11.5 Mbps for upload. The upper end is very fast, but you should realize that mobile broadband is dependent on the strength of the signal.

"Can you hear me now?" 4G is the next generation of mobile broadband. There are basically two 4G standards: LTE and WiMAX, although AT&T and T-Mobile are calling their service HSPA+ 4G. Data speeds are projected to be in the 100–326 Mbps range. Obviously, this is exponentially faster than 3G, hence, the reason the cellular companies are pitching their 4G service wherever possible.

WiMAX (Worldwide Interoperability for Microwave Access)

WiMAX is a wireless technology for delivering Internet access wirelessly at distances of up to 30 miles, far greater than the 100 feet range of Wi-Fi. Data speeds go as high as 75 Mbps. This is considered the new 4G standard, and many cellular companies have partnered to bring WiMAX to mobile phones. The technology has a low cost of implementation but still lacks market penetration due to the debate over placing the required hardware on existing towers.

Satellite

Although it seemed like a promising technology for broadband access, satellite broadband should only be used when other forms of broadband connection are not available because the speed is extremely slow, particularly for upload speeds, and the signal is affected by environmental conditions, such as weather.

How to Determine What You Need

Before you go shopping for your broadband service, you need to establish some parameters for what you need to run your office effectively. The following are some of the key factors that will affect your requirements.

The Number of Users Working in Your Office

This is one of the most important factors because a direct correlation exists between the number of users and the amount of bandwidth that you will require. The challenge is trying to figure how much bandwidth each person will need. This is greatly affected by what applications they are using throughout the day and whether the applications are on in-house servers or accessed via the cloud. It is prudent to assume that they will be evolving to cloud applications over time, which will result in a much greater need for bandwidth.

You also need to consider whether you will have remote users accessing your internal infrastructure via the Internet and whether they will be running internal applications or simply using your network as a gateway back to the cloud applications.

Number and Type of Cloud Applications

Accessing the Internet significantly affects your bandwidth requirements. Simple browsing of the Internet requires relatively little bandwidth. However, running applications over the Internet can increase your requirements significantly. For example, an organization that has an Internet-based document management system (cloud application) will be saving and retrieving files over the Internet. This means they need to consider both download and upload speeds of their Internet connection, especially if they are saving large files into the document management system.

There could be other cloud applications that have relatively small bandwidth requirements, such as an order entry system. It is best to discuss bandwidth requirements with all your cloud application vendors. More importantly, talk with other users to find out what their experience has been and the bandwidth they have in place.

Size and Type of Data Transmitted

When determining bandwidth requirements, you also need to evaluate the type of data that will be transmitted over the Internet. The largest files are typically multimedia files. The size of picture files pales in comparison to audio and video files. In addition, if your document files contain pictures, their size can grow to be very large as well. Realize that the world of information exchange is moving from being primarily text based toward more graphic and video based, so plan for significant increases in bandwidth requirements over the long term.

Upload Versus Download Speed

As discussed in the section on Internet connection types, there is one speed rating for downloads and a separate one for uploads. Downloading is pulling something from the Internet, such as when you retrieve a file from a document management system. Uploading is putting something on the Internet, such as when you save a file to a document management system. Most Internet connections have a faster speed for downloading due to the fact that people are typically downloading much more than uploading. Therefore, the broadband service providers have designed their systems to allocate more bandwidth for downloading to match the demand. However, today, the proliferation of file saving systems on the Internet means that more and more users are beginning to save files on the Internet rather than their local computers. If you get an Internet connection with a fast download speed but a slow upload speed, that means you can retrieve files quickly, but it may take significantly longer to save the files.

Thick Client Versus Thin Client

Cloud applications can work in one of two ways. *Thick client* means the actual program and data resides on the local computer when the application is active, but stored remotely, via the cloud when not in use. (There is much more technology involved than this simple explanation, but our goal is to keep it simple.) This means that every time the application is used, some or all the data must be copied or moved to the local computer before the application will run. You will need good download speed if this is the case. Also, when you are done using the application, all the updated data must be sent back to the cloud, which increases your upload speed requirements.

Thin client means the actual program and data reside on the server in the cloud, and just a small application resides on the local computer in order to make connection with the server. When using a thin client, all processing and calculations are performed at the other end of the cloud on high performance servers. The local computer simply receives screen refreshes. This process prevents large amounts of data from being transmitted and reduces the bandwidth requirements significantly. Determining whether an application is a thick or thin client design should be part of your software selection criteria.

Phone System

Many phone systems today reside on the same network as your computers and will often share the same Internet connection. Fortunately, phone systems use relatively low amounts of bandwidth, and most organizations see limited effects of adding phone systems to the Internet connection. However, it is important to realize that the nature of digital phone communications requires as much upload bandwidth as download, so take this into account when choosing your service.

When your connection is made and you have access to the Internet, you should perform a speed test to ensure you are getting the Internet speed you are paying for. A common website to perform the test is www.speedtest.net (see figures 4-2 and 4-3). Depending on your connection type, the time of day may affect your speed.

Figure 4-2: *Speed Test—AT&T DSL Service (www.speedtest.net)*

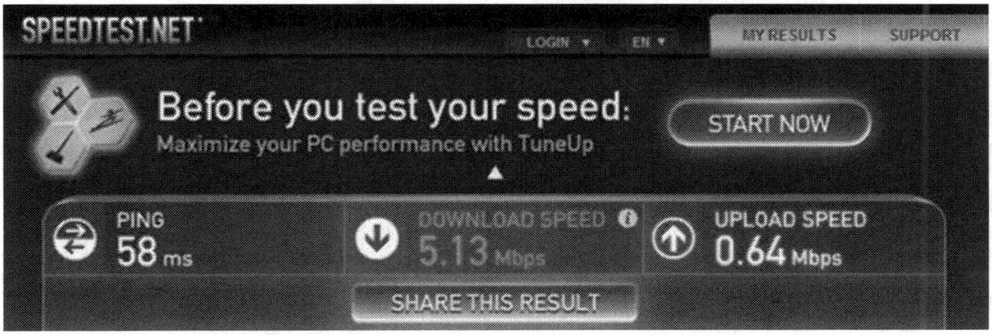

Source: Used with permission from Speedtest.net.

Figure 4-3: *Speed Test—Comcast Cable Business Class Service (www.speedtest.net)*

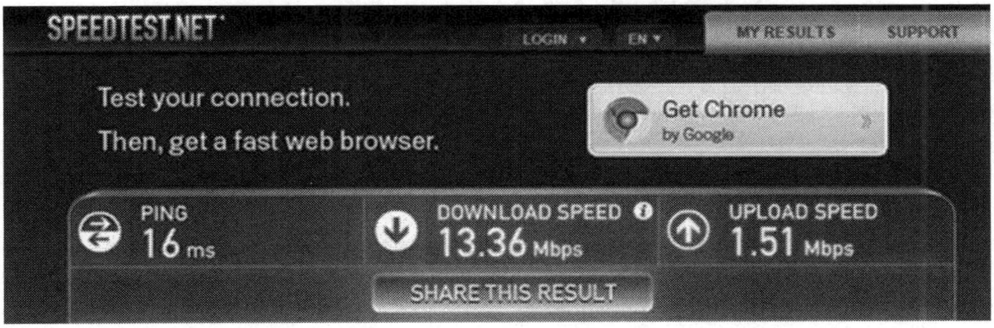

Source: Used with permission from Speedtest.net.

Where to Get Your Broadband

Plenty of service providers are available to choose from when it comes to acquiring your broadband service, and it is definitely worth your time to do some comparison shopping. Just be careful not to focus too heavily on the cost; there is too much at stake. The order of priority should be reliability, speed, and then cost. Do you remember our discussion earlier about the transformation of the IT paradigm that is dominating today—outsourcing infrastructure via the cloud? This means that the allocation of your financial resources has to be reprioritized. Bandwidth, your pipeline to the cloud, is one of your most important IT investments in this new paradigm.

The major bandwidth service providers fall into four basic categories: telephone company, cable, cellular, and regional.

Telephone Company

Most, if not all, telephone carriers provide some form of Internet connectivity, typically DSL and T1. Many are branching out into cable and cellular as well. At one time, telephone companies were the only means for Internet access due to the amount of copper wire that exists in most households and businesses.

Cable

Cable companies originally provided only TV service but soon invented technology that allowed for data traffic on their coaxial cable network. Today, most cable companies provide Internet access to both households and businesses. However, in some areas, cable companies only provide Internet access to businesses that procure TV service, such as bars and restaurants.

Cellular

Cellular coverage used to be available only in metropolitan areas. Today, cellular coverage is available throughout the United States, and only sparsely populated areas are still without coverage. The cellular signal was originally intended exclusively for phone service. However, like most other phone service providers, cellular companies developed technology to provide digital transmission along with analog and voice transmission. This means that any area covered by cellular voice is usually covered by cellular data as well.

Regional

Regionally, there are a variety of other providers of broadband Internet access, including governments, technology companies, and nonprofit organizations.

So the $64,000 question is from whom should I procure my bandwidth? The answer is likely to evolve pretty naturally. You need to research the available options in your geographical area. Box 4-1 outlines the steps you should take to evaluate and select your broadband service.

Box 4-1: *Broadband Procurement Checklist*

- Research available service providers in your geographic area: telephone company, cable, cellular, and regional. Priority should be given to the telephone company and cable for a wired connection. Cellular is more appropriate for back-up service.
- Gather upload and download speed ratings for each of the available service providers. Most carriers today offer multiple tiers of service. You will pay for speed!
- Obtain pricing proposals from the appropriately qualified service providers.
- Develop a matrix that compares the speed and prices of the alternative service providers.
- Based on the speed and price analysis, contact the providers' customer references that meet your speed requirements to assess the performance, reliability, and customer service record.
- Procure the preferred service as well as a back-up service provider.
- Conduct multiple speed tests (www.speedtest.net) while the service provider is on site to make sure you are getting the bandwidth you signed up for.

Recommendations

The following are some additional tips that will help you procure your bandwidth:

Contact Vendors

Check with your building management company to determine if they know who provides service. If you are in a newer building, then special arrangements may have been made during construction to provide high speed Internet via a specific carrier. If you are in a multitenant building, ask other tenants what they are using and their level of satisfaction. You can also contact your local telephone company and cable company.

Main Communications Network

Based on your bandwidth requirements, you should select the vendor that meets your needs within your budget. During your evaluation, you should talk to other businesses that are using the vendor and solution. Make sure to ask the vendor to provide references of businesses of similar size and Internet usage in your local area. Procure multiple quotes, not only to force competitive pricing, but also to help educate yourself on this topic. Each vendor will provide valuable information about Internet connection at your location for comparison purposes.

Back-up Communications Network

As you become more reliant on your Internet connection, you should consider a backup or secondary Internet connection source. This connection does not need to be a complete duplicate of your primary service because it should only be used if that service fails. This should be an infrequent occurrence if you have done your homework to find the correct provider. However, failures do occur, and this back-up connection may be slower, but it will allow your organization to have continuous Internet access and keep your operations running.

If, or when, you consider moving into a new building, it is important to evaluate the Internet capabilities of the building. Some older buildings have limited connectivity options and, if you require service that is not available, you may have to pay additional fees to have the service brought into the building. This could cost thousands of dollars. If you are constructing a building, make sure you consider the Internet connectivity in the area where you will be building. Then make sure the cost of construction includes getting the necessary broadband service into the building.

Two Alternative Approaches

If you are typical of many small firm practitioners, you are probably trying to manage your firm in between the cracks of servicing your clients throughout the day. So you do not have a lot of time or inclination to become a data communications expert, but you want to make a prudent choice for your firm. With that in mind, we offer two alternative approaches to resolving your broadband needs:

1. Contact three broadband vendors in your local area: cable, telephone company, and others if available. Ask them to visit your office and help you calculate your requirements. Evaluate their proposals in terms of speeds promised, costs, and quality of service (based on talking with other customers in your area.)
2. Contact a minimum of three practitioners in your local area. Get a sense of how heavily they are accessing the Internet, what broadband service they are using, and what their assessment is of the performance and reliability. Choose the best provider based on this research.

Table 4-1 shows a sample of broadband cable for business from Comcast and, for DSL, from AT&T.

Table 4-1: *Cable vs. DSL Comparison*

Comcast Broadband Cable Internet Service for Business				
Service	Starter	Premium	Deluxe	Deluxe 100
Price (per month)	$99	$140	$230	$410
Download Speed (Mbps)	12	14	32	64
Upload Speed (Mbps)	2	5	10	10
Phone line included	✓	✓	✓	✓

AT&T Broadband DSL Internet Service for Business				
Service	Small Office/Home Office DSL		Business Class DSL	
Price (per month)	$55	$65	$70	$80
Download Speed (Mbps)	3	6	3	6
Upload Speed *(Kbps)	512*	768*	512*	768*
IP Addresses	1	1	29	29

Note: This table is not intended to promote Comcast and AT&T over other providers. It is simply a good benchmark for you to compare national service providers.

Broadband to Go

With the proliferation of smartphones and tablets, the need for wireless broadband has grown exponentially in recent years. The good news is that the cellular broadband speeds have improved significantly with the new 4G service described previously. It is very easy to compare the service offerings from the major carriers, AT&T, Sprint, and Verizon, as well as the regional carriers. Box 4-2 points out a few key things to look for when shopping for wireless broadband.

Box 4-2: *Cellular Broadband Checklist*

- Is 4G service available in your local area?
- What is the data transfer limit and surcharge, if any?
- How long do you have to lock into a contract?
- Are you buying for a specific device, that is, phone or tablet, or a hotspot?
- Is there a volume discount for multiple accounts?
- Can you use your smartphone as a hotspot to feed Wi-Fi to other devices?
- How many simultaneous connections can the hotspot service?

Hotspots

Here is a little tutorial on hotspots. A *hotspot* is simply a device that delivers Wi-Fi service to other devices. When you walk into Starbucks and connect to their Wi-Fi service, you are connecting to a hotspot. All the major cell phone service providers offer plans that enable most smartphones to function as a hotspot for your other personal devices, such as your laptop and iPad. These services tend to cost about $30 per month and often have a limit on how much data can be transmitted back and forth to your device during the month (see table 4-2). If you go over that limit, you will incur a surcharge. On the other hand, you may find a provider that offers unlimited data for a flat monthly fee. The key here is to read the fine print in the service agreement about what the fees are and what is included. If you do not have a smartphone, you can purchase a mobile hotspot or Mi-Fi device. These devices require a cellular service contract similar to your smartphone and will provide Wi-Fi service to multiple devices simultaneously. Many practitioners use this approach to provide staff with Internet service when they are working in the field.

Table 4-2: *Mobile Broadband Service Plans**

Carrier	Sprint		AT&T	Verizon	
Price (monthly)	$35	$80	$50	$50	$80
Data Limits	3 GB	12 GB	5 GB	5 GB	10 GB
Additional Data Surcharge	5¢ per additional MB		$10 per additional GB	$10 per additional GB	
Other	$10 premium data add on for smartphone				

* *Note:* These data carrier plans are changing on a regular basis. Be sure to read the fine print on all service contracts and research the speed and reliability levels for your area.

An important decision for you to make when purchasing a tablet is whether to subscribe to the cellular data service plan that delivers Wi-Fi directly to the device, purchase the hotspot service through your smartphone, or purchase a stand-alone Mi-Fi hotspot device. The latter option offers you the most flexibility.

Chapter 5

The CPA Technology Toolkit

The CPA Technology Toolkit is our recommended collection of the hardware and software tools that you need to outfit your staff with on an individual basis. This includes desktops and laptops, tablets, smartphones, Microsoft Office, Adobe Acrobat, and so forth. We will provide a detailed blueprint that will put you in a position to achieve maximum productivity by leveraging the most cost-effective solutions (see figure 5-1 for an overview). We have tried to make the point throughout this book to not be penny wise and pound foolish with these tools. Your staff time is too valuable and comes at a high price, so anything you can do to maximize their productivity will benefit all concerned. The investment payback on these items is typically measured in months, not years.

Figure 5-1: *CPA Technology Toolkit Components*

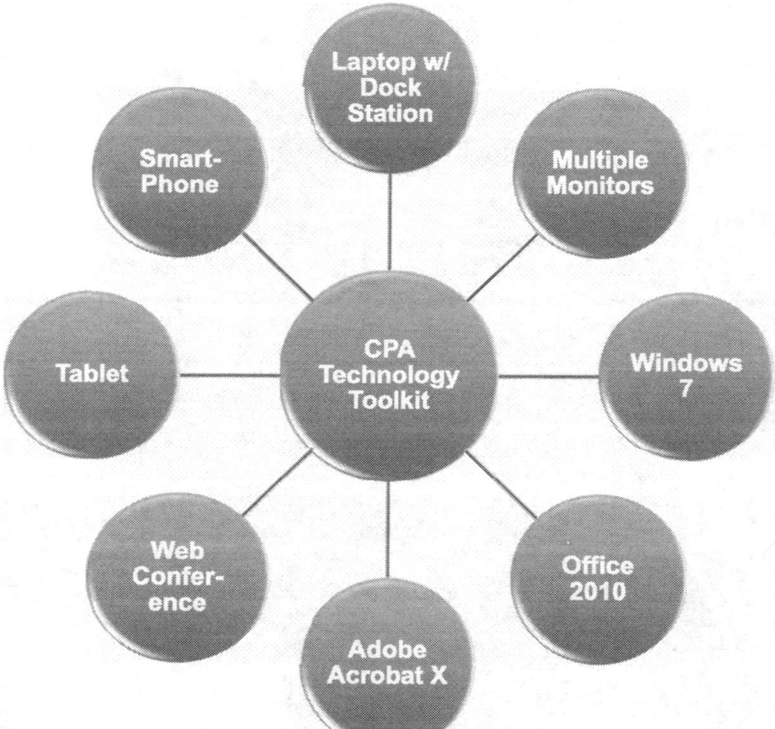

Desktop Computer Versus Laptop

This is always one of the most important decisions you have to make in regards to outfitting your staff. Our recommendation is that all your client service delivery personnel should be equipped with a high performance, lightweight laptop with a full-featured docking station. This provides maximum flexibility and usability. It allows you to implement stronger mobile computing security controls because they are using the same device in and out of the office, and it is under your ownership and control. You can eliminate the option of allowing them to connect to your applications with their personal equipment, which brings a whole new level of issues regarding policies and procedures. For your support staff, which you typically do not expect or require to work remotely, a desktop computer is suitable because the overall workstation cost will be less than a laptop configuration. The exception would be for any support staff that are set up for telecommuting.

Recommended Desktop and Laptop Configuration

One thing to be aware of in relation to this is that most hardware manufacturers provide two types of computers: a consumer model and a business model. There may be other specialty models for particular uses, for example, medical, outdoor, rugged, and so forth. The consumer models are targeted toward the consumer market in which the buyer is likely to be more price conscious. These computers have the least costly components, and the quality fluctuates over time. The manufacturer's goal is to build a quality computer for the least cost. These computers often have the latest in graphics cards in order to serve the gaming and DVD market. For Dell, these product lines include Inspiron and XPS. For Lenovo (formerly IBM), these would be the IdeaPad, IdeaCentre, and Essential lines. For Hewlett Packard (HP), these would be the Pavilion line.

The business product lines are targeted toward the business market in which the buyer may be price conscious but is also concerned about quality, performance, and longevity. Most businesses have multiple computers and usually do not purchase them all at the same time. But from a support standpoint, they want to make sure that if they purchase the same model, it is exactly like the one purchased previously. This helps with supporting the deployment of computers throughout the office. There is less concern about high-end gaming graphics cards than there is for all the machines having the same graphics card. For Dell, these business lines are the Latitude, Precision, and OptiPlex. For Lenovo, these would be the ThinkPad, ThinkCentre, or ThinkStation. For HP, these would be ProBook, EliteBook, 500, and Pro line.

As a side note, make sure you take advantage of any discounts when purchasing your PC such as the discounts available through the AICPA's affinity programs. We suggest applying some of the savings you receive through discounts to purchase a three year extended on-site warranty.

The following is a checklist of the key specifications to look for in desktop and laptop computers. The highest performance options are marked with an asterisk.

- **Processor:** Intel model i3, i5, i7* or AMD model Phenom II or Athlon II.*
- **Disk storage:** 250–320 GB hard drive at 7,200 RPM speed or solid state drive (SSD).* The solid state drives are significantly more expensive. However, they affect overall performance substantially, and prices are expected to start dropping significantly in 2012.
- **RAM memory:** 4 MB or 8 MB.* We recommend that all of your newly purchased computers be equipped with 8 MB of RAM.

- **Graphics card:** You should opt for a dual graphics card because it will support up to four monitors attached to the unit. In the case of laptops, be sure there is an external visual graphics adapter (VGA) or HDMI port to connect a second external monitor.
- **USB ports:** Multiple USB ports are mandatory because nearly all peripheral devices are designed to connect with the USB port. The current standard is USB 2.0, but USB 3.0 is now on the market and provides speeds that are rated at 10 times faster than the 2.0 standard. This is one of those specifications that will help extend the longevity of your computer because 3.0 is sure to be the standard that all peripheral devices, such as external disks, printers, and scanners, will be designed to leverage over the next few years. The good news is that they are backward compatible; therefore, there is no downside to using the 3.0 standard.
- **Integrated camera (laptop):** This is not going to jump out at you as a "must have" component today. But we feel confident in saying the integration of video conferencing into our business models is poised for significant growth in the coming years, with tools such as Skype, FaceTime, GoToMeeting, and so forth. You do not want the lack of an integrated camera to be the item that renders your laptop obsolete in a year or two. This is not an issue with desktops because you can always procure a stand-alone camera when the time calls for it.
- **Docking station (laptop):** We highly recommend that you deploy a full-featured docking station (see figure 5-2) with an external keyboard, mouse, and dual or triple monitors. The docking station should have at least two or three USB ports and dual video ports to support connecting two external monitors. There are many different types of video ports available, including VGA and digital visual interface (DVI). You also want to verify that the docking station has audio in/out jacks and an ethernet port for a wired network connection. The benefit of this setup is that the user can simply slide his or her laptop in and out of the docking station without opening the display lid. This means that you can purchase a lightweight laptop with a smaller display for better mobility because you will have the larger external monitors that offer compatible display resolutions and size when working in the office.

Figure 5-2: *Dell Full-Featured Docking Station*

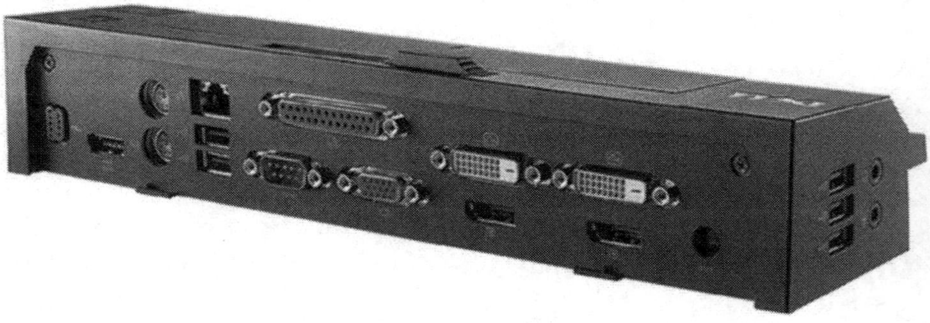

Source: Used with Permission from Dell. © Dell 2012 Inc. All Rights Reserved.

Multiple Monitors

One of your greatest productivity gains will come from the use of multiple monitors (see figure 5-3). This allows you to have multiple programs open at one time and see them on the various monitors simultaneously versus finding them on the task bar in Windows and constantly maximizing, minimizing, and sizing them. This means a user can have MS Outlook on one monitor, tax software on another, and a PDF file of the supporting documents on a third monitor. If you have not invested in dual or triple monitors yet, this should be at the top of the list of priorities because the return on investment begins immediately with a boost in your personal productivity.

In order to deploy multiple monitors, the desktop or laptop must have the required video components. This is a two-fold issue: a physical connection and the video capabilities. When purchasing your computers, verify the number of monitors that can be connected. We also recommend you test this to the maximum capabilities even if you do not initially plan on using the maximum number supported. This is because it may not be readily apparent that you need additional hardware.

On desktops, the actual graphics card will have multiple ports, or they may provide a dongle that connects to the graphics port and has multiple ports on the dongle that your monitor cables connect to. Make sure the necessary cables or dongles are included with the system because they can be somewhat costly when purchased separately.

On laptops, the graphics card usually comes with an external VGA port, but more and more hardware providers are including HDMI or DisplayPort interfaces. You need to make sure you are aware what ports your desktops and laptops support when you purchase your monitors. Typically, a laptop will support at least two monitors, the built-in display, and an external monitor. Refer back to our recommendation that you purchase a full-featured docking station that can support at least two external monitors, so that you can keep the laptop lid closed when it is placed in the docking station.

If your system or docking station has only one or two external monitor ports built in, you can connect additional monitors through special USB connections. Examples of these are provided in appendix C, "Resource Center."

Figure 5-3: *Dual Monitor Configuration With Stand*

Selecting Monitors and Accessories

A single, large screen monitor is not the optimal solution. Instead of one big 30-inch monitor, for instance, you are better off with 2, 21-inch monitors because in a window environment, it is much more efficient to maximize windows on two separate monitors versus sizing the windows to fit on one monitor. The time saved avoiding this task alone can justify the cost of the second monitor. The two most important criteria in selecting your monitors are the size and display quality. As mentioned previously, for size, we recommend 21-inch monitors. If you are going to deploy a triple monitor solution, the third should be 23 inches, so that you can mount it in portrait mode for viewing full page documents from top to bottom. Regarding the quality of the display, refer to the discussion of liquid crystal display (LCD) and light-emitting diode (LED) that follows. An important point to remember is that you should always set your monitor's resolution to the native setting. This will ensure the highest quality display possible. All too often, practitioners will adjust the resolution to a very high setting. This will result in a display that is of a lower quality than the monitor is capable of.

The monitors connect to the computer via a cable attached to a specific port. Make sure the monitor has the ports required by your computer. They include VGA, DVI, DisplayPort (USB connection), and HDMI. Traditionally, the most popular port has been the VGA. However, the market is rapidly transitioning to DVI, DisplayPort, and HDMI. The bottom line is to make sure your computer or docking station supports the monitor's ports.

Some additional specifications should be considered. There are two basic types of monitors: LCD and LED. Do not be confused because an LED monitor is actually an LCD monitor with different backlighting. We will not get into the technical aspects, but realize that monitors may be advertised as LCD, LED, or LED LCD. For the most part, LED and LED LCD are the same. Having said all that, we recommend LED monitors because they are brighter, easier on the eyes, use less power, and are more environmentally friendly when disposed.

Consider a monitor that rotates, so you can use it in portrait mode versus the typical landscape mode. Portrait mode is great for viewing documents and web pages, whereas landscape is good for spreadsheets. There are many different mounting stands available with a universal bracket (for example, see figure 5-4). Find one that suits your preferences. Consider the monitor's ergonomic adjustment capabilities, especially if you are going to use the built-in stand. Things to look at are height, tilt, swivel, and angle adjustments.

Figure 5-4: *Universal Mounting Bracket for Quad Monitors (Ergotron DS100)*

Source: Used with permission from Ergotron, Inc.

There are all kinds of other technical specifications, such as contrast ratio, refresh rates, panel types, pixel pitch, color support, and so forth. However, unless you need a monitor for multimedia development or gaming, most of these specifications are not as important as the others we discussed, especially for an accounting and tax practice.

Windows® 7

Source: Used with permission from Microsoft.

When you purchase a desktop or laptop today, you have essentially two operating platforms to choose from: Microsoft® Windows and Apple Mac OS®. The accounting, tax, and other business applications software that you are going to use in your practice are overwhelmingly designed for the Windows platform. Therefore, this is the more practical choice in terms of ensuring that your hardware will be compatible with your software applications, and you minimize compatibility issues. Therefore, Windows is our recommended platform for CPA practices. In a later chapter, we will talk about the iPad. In our opinion, the best way to experience the Apple environment is as a supplement to your Windows computer.

Having said that, the Apple MacBook line of computers has become increasingly popular because of the Apple interface and sleek design. Also, there are various ways to get most of your Windows applications to run through the MacBook. However, this sometimes requires jumping through several of hoops, and the market for supporting Windows applications running on a MacBook is more limited. The bottom line is, if you want to use a MacBook, be sure you thoroughly investigate the compatibility with all the mission critical applications you need to run: Exchange Server, tax, accounting, working paper software, and so forth. This research should include talking with other practitioners who are actually using the same applications via the MacBook. The good news is that the more you utilize cloud-based applications that are truly browser based, that is, designed to run through your browser, the easier it is to use the MacBook. However, we stand by our recommendation for Windows as your primary platform.

Now that we have cleared the air on that topic, let's turn to a discussion of Windows 7. First, we think it is fair to say that Windows 7 is, by far, the best Windows operating system that Microsoft has produced. It is faster, more reliable, and more flexible than all its predecessors. We can only hope that Windows 8 will be improved even further. Our recommendation is that if you have any desktops or laptops running XP or Vista, then it is time to cycle those units out and replace them with new devices that have Windows 7 installed. This will bring your desktops and laptops up to current standards, and you will be impressed with the improvement in both speed and reliability. Remember, our main premise is that your staff's time is too valuable to be spent waiting on the computer.

A few points about Windows 7 need to be addressed. Most computers you purchase today will have Windows 7 preinstalled. However, there are important differences between the different editions of Windows 7. Recall our recommendation to stay away from the consumer models of desktops and laptops and procure the business models. Well, this is one of the reasons. There are three Windows 7 versions: Home Premium, Professional, and Ultimate. Without getting into the technical differences, the Home Premium version is not acceptable if you are going to connect your computer to a network.

Another consideration is whether to deploy Windows 7 in 32 bit or 64 bit mode. If Windows 7 is preinstalled on your new computer, then the choice will have been made for you. Otherwise, you should deploy in 64 bit mode for better performance that will take advantage of the 64 bit processors. The only caveat is that if you will be connecting older peripheral devices or running older software applications, they may be incompatible with the 64 bit operating system. Be sure to investigate the compatibility of all your devices and software before you buy. Nothing is more frustrating, time consuming, and costly than buying and configuring a new computer, only to discover that there are some critical incompatibility issues. If you discover some, our recommendation is to upgrade the device or software.

It is time to come into the Windows 7 platform. It is mature, and the performance and reliability gains will provide a relatively quick return on your investment.

Microsoft® Office

Source: Used with permission from Microsoft.

Microsoft Office has earned the distinction of being the predominant personal productivity software suite over the past 20 years. The current version is Office 2010, which sold more than 100 million user licenses in its first year on the market. Therefore, we do not think we need to spend much time making the case for using MS Office as a standard (see the section, "Google Apps" that follows.) In the software market, there is definitely safety in numbers as more and more businesses come to rely on an application such as MS Office. There is much greater incentive for the vendors to continually work toward improving the application's features, functions, and reliability.

The current generation of MS Office was ushered in with MS Office 2007 and the introduction of the revolutionary ribbon interface that replaced the traditional command menus and toolbars (see figure 5-5). The interface definitely takes some time to get used to. However, most experienced users will agree that it is a much more efficient interface. Every function throughout the MS Office 2010 suite is virtually just two or three clicks away. This new interface was carried forward from MS Office 2007 to 2010, and every indication is that this format is going to be around for quite a while. In fact, you will find that many other software developers are emulating this same interface for their applications.

Figure 5-5: *MS Office 2010 Ribbon Interface*

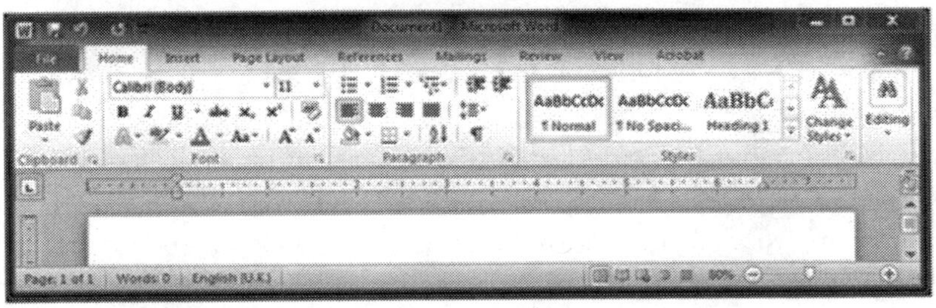

Source: Used with permission from Microsoft.

We recommend that you upgrade to the MS Office 2010 suite as soon as it is practical for you if you are still using MS Office 2003 or an earlier version. The productivity gains you will achieve from the enhanced functionality and stability will return your investment in a matter of months. If you are currently using MS Office 2007, there is no compelling reason to upgrade immediately because there are only incremental improvements from Office 2007 to 2010. The one exception is Outlook. It has been improved significantly between the two releases.

With MS Office 2010, you have the option of implementing the 32 bit or 64 bit version. From a performance perspective, the 64 bit version will be faster. However, you are more likely to run into compatibility issues with other applications that integrate with MS Office. The more conservative option is to deploy the 32 bit version. If you are intent on the 64 bit version, be sure to contact all your software vendors whose applications will be integrated with the MS Office applications to make sure there are no compatibility issues with the 64 bit version. Also, be aware that you can install the 32 bit version of MS Office on a computer that is running the 64 bit version of Windows. They do not need to be the same. There are three MS Office suite bundles to choose from: Student, Home & Business, and Professional. The student version is not licensed to be used in business. For most businesses, the Home & Business suite should be used. This bundle includes Excel, OneNote, Outlook, PowerPoint, and Word. The Professional suite includes two additional applications: Access and Publisher. For the vast majority of practitioners, the Home & Business bundle is all that is required. You can mix and match suites, that is, you do not need the same suite on all workstations; you can have Home & Business on some, and Professional on others. If you need to purchase five or more licenses, Microsoft offers a volume discount, which can be purchased through an authorized distributor. You have the option to purchase one license for one user on one computer or one license for one user on two computers for a relatively small price increase.

Microsoft Office From the Cloud

You know the cloud is for real when Microsoft makes the strategic decision to deploy a version of the MS Office applications over the Internet. In 2010, Microsoft launched Office 365, which is a set of cloud-based applications that include Office Professional Plus, SharePoint Online, Exchange Online, Office Web Apps, and Lync Online. Visit Microsoft's website for more information on each of these applications. Unlike the retail and volume license products, which are considered desktop applications because they are installed on a local computer, MS Office 365 provides a subscription service based on a per user, per month pricing model. As with all software as a service (SaaS) applications, MS Office 365 includes not only the software license but also the server infrastructure and network administration services to support it. Think about the benefits of being able to access your MS Office applications from anywhere, at any time, from virtually any computer. You do not have to run it from "your" dedicated machine. Also, you will always be on the current version of Office. No more struggling with the cost and effort required to upgrade from one release to the next.

Google Apps™

Google Apps™ service is a cloud/SaaS based bundle of applications designed to compete directly with Microsoft Office. Google Apps includes Web-based e-mail, calendar, and Google Docs. The latter is an application that is a bundle of applications, including word processing, presentations, and spreadsheets. Prior to the release of MS Office 365, Google Apps was garnering a slice of the MS Office market because it offered distinct advantages as a cloud-based application that the traditional desktop version of MS Office could not provide. Those advantages fade away when comparing Google Apps to MS Office 365. If you research the Internet for discussions about these two competing application services, you will typically find that on a feature by feature basis, they are fairly comparable. The huge advantage that MS Office has is the depth of its installed base of users and the breadth of integration with third party applications, including accounting and tax software. For these reasons, we think that MS Office is the more practical solution for most accounting and tax practices. You also have to take into consideration the depth of experienced MS Office users that exist in the marketplace. It is much easier to recruit an accounting and tax professional who is well versed in the MS Office applications as compared to Google Apps.

Adobe® Acrobat®

Adobe® Acrobat® X

Source: Adobe product box shot reprinted with permission from Adobe Systems Incorporated.

One of the most fundamental attributes of a digital practice model is the conversion of all paper documents and reports to digital format. Adobe Systems, Inc. saw the future of this transformation back in 1993 when they developed the PDF (portable document format) for storing documents and reports as electronic images. The PDF format is an open standard, which means any software developer can create applications that can create, view, edit, and annotate PDF formatted files. Adobe System's strategic objective was to be the primary source of software applications for creating and working with PDFs. Adobe Acrobat software originated from there and, over the past 20 years, Acrobat has emerged as the undisputed market leader. Although there are other applications, often at a lower price, Adobe's value as a market leader has also established a level of standardization in the PDF software market, much like MS Office has done in the spreadsheet and word processing market.

In our opinion, Adobe Acrobat should be a standard part of every CPAs toolkit. Most people are familiar with the free version called Adobe Reader. The strategy behind Adobe Reader is to eliminate any objections to the use of the PDF format. With the free version of Reader, anyone can open and view a PDF file. If you want to create PDF files, annotate them, secure them, and more, you will need the full Adobe Acrobat software. The current release is Acrobat X (10). For better or for worse, Adobe made a significant change in the user interface in Acrobat X from its predecessor. As with the transition from MS Office 2003 to 2007/2010, it will take some time to learn the new Acrobat X interface but, ultimately, you are likely to find the Acrobat X interface more efficient.

There are two versions of Adobe Acrobat: Standard and Pro. The Standard version retails for approximately $280, and the Pro version is priced at $420. We recommend that you equip all staff who will be working with PDF files with Acrobat Standard. The Pro version offers a number of additional features, which you can review by visiting www.adobe.com. The key features of the Pro version include the ability to apply encrypted redaction of specific information, for example, a taxpayer ID number, within a PDF file, and the ability to create and distribute electronic forms. Therefore, we recommend that you procure at least one license of Pro in the event you want to take advantage of these features in your office.

An important consideration is to make sure the Adobe Acrobat version is compatible with Microsoft Office. If you are using MS Office 2010, you will need Acrobat X in order to take advantage of the integration between the two applications.

Web Conferencing System

In chapter 13, "Developing and Implementing Your Technology Plan," we focus on how to develop and implement your plan for making the transformation to the digital practice model. One of the biggest challenges you will face is trying to determine the optimal order of priorities and the timeline. The two easiest and highly beneficial steps you can take are to deploy multiple monitors (discussed previously) and implement a web conferencing system. If you are not currently doing either of these two things, make them first on your list. You do not even have to wait until you formulate the rest of your plan because they should be considered mandatory. Through both of these initiatives, you will see real value very quickly and that is important for reinforcing why you need to consider completing all the steps outlined in this book.

So what is web conferencing? It is a lot simpler and more useful than many people realize. It is simply an application that will allow you to conduct online meetings, whereby you invite one or more participants to join via their browser by sending them a link to click on. There are many little nuances to web conferencing, but the following are the primary characteristics of these systems:

- Web conferencing systems are SaaS applications, except in rare cases.
- Pricing is typically based on a per user monthly fee to host unlimited meetings for a predetermined maximum number of participants, typically, 10, 25, 50, 100, and beyond.
- The "host" of the meeting initiates the session and invites attendees via an e-mail link, which is often in the form of a meeting invitation that can be accepted directly into their calendar application.
- Audio is provided either through a teleconference phone call or through the computer's audio. In most cases, you can give the attendees the option to call in or listen and talk via the computer.
- The primary application is for the host to share his or her computer screen to present a PowerPoint slide show, review a PDF file, walk through an Excel spreadsheet, and so forth.
- The host can make any attendee a presenter, which means he or she can show his or her computer screen to the rest of the attendees. There is no practical limit to what the presenter can show: software applications, Internet browsing, video, and so forth.
- The host can transfer control of his or her keyboard to an attendee, which allows the attendee to control the host's computer. The primary application for this feature is to provide remote support of a computer application. The classic example is to have your client give you control of his or her keyboard while you record some adjusting journal entries in his or her accounting system, rather than trying to talk them through the steps. This also allows all parties in the meeting to watch the activity on the screen.
- The use of web cameras to display video is an optional feature. It is not always necessary, but sometimes it can add a more personal touch. Do not be intimidated by this feature. We have been using web conferencing extensively in our business for the past four years and admittedly have not used the video feed very often. However, with the explosive growth in the sales of iPads and smartphones with built-in cameras and applications such as Skype™ and FaceTime®, we all need to be prepared for the age of video conferencing, which is likely to proliferate over the next few years.
- Most web conferencing systems provide the option to record the meeting, including audio. This provides you with an automatic archive of the meeting and can minimize the need to take copious notes.

The Web Conferencing Value Proposition

There are numerous web conferencing systems available (see figure 5-6 as an example). However, the four top sellers are GoToMeeting® (Citrix,) WebEx® (Cisco,) Lync® (Microsoft), and Connect™ (Adobe.) Each has its particular strengths and weaknesses, but they will all achieve the same objective. Make it a personal goal to sign up for a trial account (see appendix C, "Resource Center") with one or more of these vendors over the next 30 days and conduct a few test meetings. You can host a meeting with others within your office just to get a comfort level with the process.

Figure 5-6: *GoToMeeting® Control Panel*

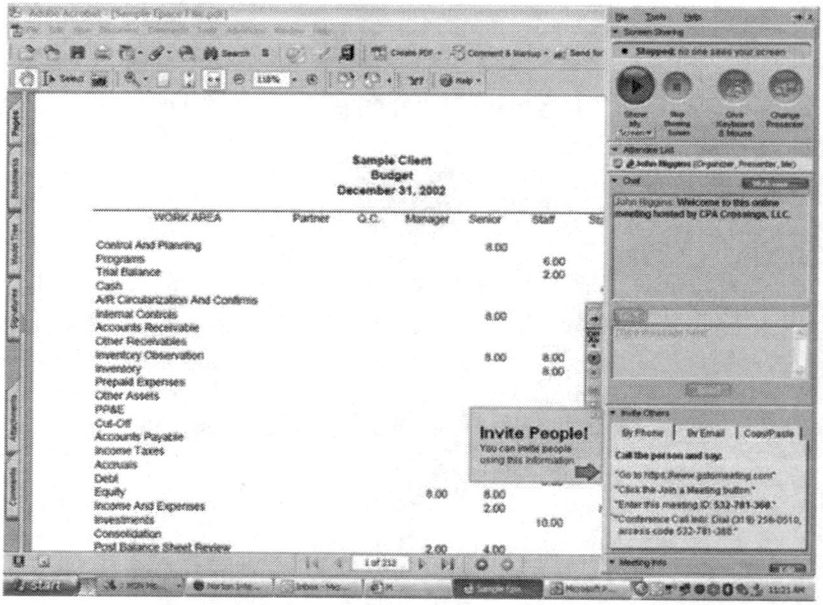

Source: Adobe product screenshot reprinted with permission from Adobe Systems Incorporated.

iPad® and Tablet

In 2010, Apple introduced the iPad®. In 2011, Apple created the iPad2, and, in 2012, the iPad 3. These simple, yet powerful devices have seen significant penetration into the accounting profession. What was designed as a consumer device has seen amazing acceptance in the business world. The power of the iPad comes from the apps. These apps will be discussed later, but these are what make the iPad able to actually perform productive work.

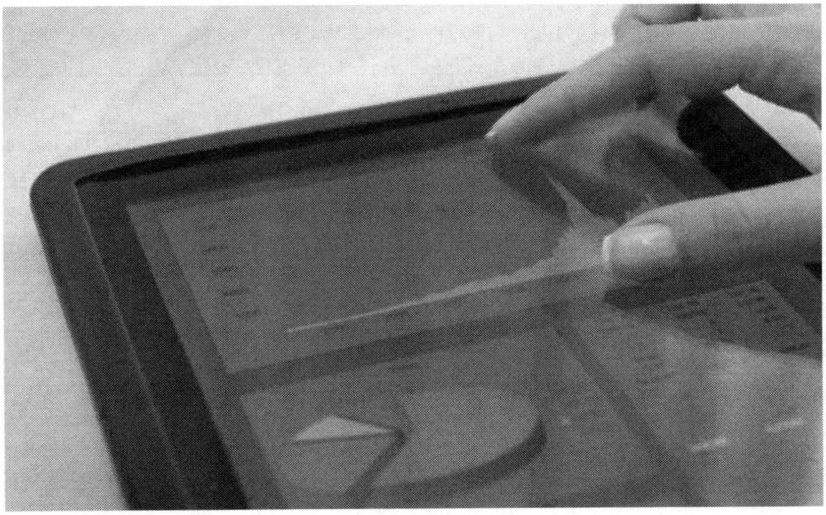

The two most frequent questions we receive about the iPad and other tablet devices are how can I use this in my practice, and what are the best apps? There are no short answers to either of these questions. There are many different ways to leverage the tablet device in a CPA practice, and there is an abundance of useful apps. Our perspective is that the iPad is a worthwhile investment for all your client service professionals, if for no other use than to leverage the portability of the device to access electronic documents wherever you go and have the ability to annotate them on the fly. Of course, there are many more applications for these devices, so your utilization will steadily increase as you discover more apps that will increase your productivity.

One of the keys to successfully deploying iPads or other tablet devices in your firm is to avoid the temptation to think that these devices can replace your desktop or laptop. Think of your computer as your production device for creating documents, spreadsheets, entering transaction data, and the like. Think of your tablet as a consumption device for viewing documents, taking notes, surfing the Internet, and participating in video conferences. There is definitely overlap between the two devices, but that is a lot better than a gap.

The Apple iPad is clearly the current gold standard in the tablet market, with an estimated 70 percent to 80 percent of the tablet market share in 2011, according to International Data Corp. If history is an indicator of the future, we are likely to see tablets based on the Android (Google) platform steadily eat into Apple's market share. This is what happened with the iPhone, which owned the market for the first couple of years after it was released, until all of the Android smartphones started to appear on the scene. As of today, the bottom line is that the iPad is the most practical tablet option simply due to its abundance of apps and user community. We will have to watch what happens to the market when the Windows 8 operating system is released. It is supposed to feature significantly enhanced support for touch technology, which is the core feature of the iPad. The big advantage Microsoft has is the ability to run the native Office applications on the tablet device. This is the single most frequent request we hear from practitioners. They want to be able to work with their spreadsheets on the iPad using the native MS Office applications.

The key to implementing tablet technology within your practice is developing a strategy for how you will integrate them into your core business processes. This may be as simple as identifying where you need access to documents and files when you are away from your desk, such as when you are meeting in the conference room or out visiting a client to discuss the financial statements. You also need to address your policies and procedures for personal versus business use. Refer to our discussion of this with smartphones that follows. The policies should be applied consistently across both devices because they are so similar in the issues that need to be addressed.

Smartphones

In order to complete the cycle in the CPA toolkit bundle, we need to discuss smartphones. These have become such an integral part of everyday life. You need to decide how to address them in your firm. The key issues you need to address include the following:

1. Will the firm purchase these for employees for asset control purposes?
2. If not, will employees be allowed to enable their devices to access firm e-mail, applications, and data?
3. How will you secure these devices in the event they are lost or stolen?

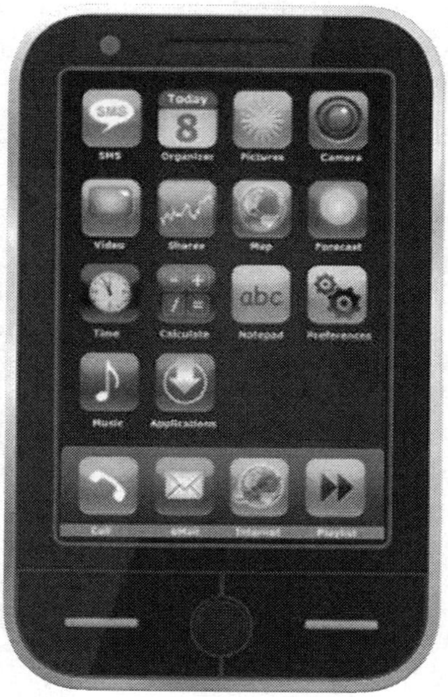

Our recommendation is that you begin by determining your strategy for mobile computing. You first need to decide the degree to which you want to embrace the use of both tablets and smartphones. One of the key advantages of proactively using these devices is that they allow your staff to be more responsive to clients by having access to e-mail at virtually anytime, and in the case of the phones, to receive and return client calls more promptly. In this day and age, it is also a sign to your clients that you are embracing current technologies. One reasonable strategy is to deploy tablets as an extension of the desktop or laptop, at least as much as practical, for accessing e-mail, applications, and documents, and limit the use of cell phones to voice and e-mail communications. This provides you with greater opportunity to implement the appropriate security measures when accessing the firm's applications and data by keeping the tablet 100 percent under the firm's control. It is much less practical to limit the use of the cell phone for firm business only, but if you limit the ability to connect the phone to the firm's applications and data, there is a much smaller possibility that the staff's personal use will result in a breach of privacy or unauthorized access of client information.

If you make the decision to deploy smartphones or tablets, or both, we offer the following recommendations regarding policies and procedures:

- The firm should purchase the devices in order to have full control over the policies and procedures for usage and to take physical control of the device and content at will.
- Because you will control ownership, you should standardize the specific equipment and not make exceptions for certain people to have different models. Each time you introduce a different model, you double the effort required to secure and support the devices.
- Prohibit the use of the device for personal use; no personal apps or e-mail accounts.
- In the case of the smartphone, allow personal phone calls from a practical perspective. However, strictly prohibit using the phone in any manner while driving.
- Set up passcode security on the phone to prevent unauthorized access to the phone and, indirectly, to firm e-mail, applications, and data.
- Establish a process to remotely wipe the contents of the device in the event that it is lost, stolen, or the employee is terminated.
- Clearly communicate to staff that because the firm owns the device, you have every right to control its usage and view any and all content.
- The key is to send a clear and strong message that the devices are not for personal use.

Picking Your Platform and Device

There are two primary decisions you have to make regarding your deployment of smartphones and tablets: the platform and the device. We already discussed the fact that the iPad is currently the de facto standard in tablets. Therefore, our discussion here will focus on the smartphones.

There are four primary platforms in the smartphone market: Apple iOS (iPhone®), Google Android™, Microsoft Windows Mobile, and RIM Blackberry®. They have all had their time at the top and, currently, Android is leading in market share. The major platforms are highlighted in figure 5-7.

Figure 5-7: *The Big Four Smartphone Platforms*

Android™

This platform was developed by Google and currently has the largest share of the market of the big four in terms of devices operating on this platform. This is due in large part to the more open architecture of the Android that allows it to be deployed on many different phone models provided by numerous manufacturers, such as HTC, Samsung, and Motorola.

The Android apps market is on par with the Apple iPhone, and these bring a great deal of additional utility to these devices. One of the drawbacks to the Android platform is that there are many hands in the development and support chain. Google develops the operating system, the phone manufacturers provide the hardware and tweak the system to meet some of their unique requirements, and the cellular companies provide the service. The result is that Android phones are not completely consistent or standardized across the different devices, opposite of the Apple model. Android supports both physical and virtual keyboards, which offers greater flexibility.

Apple iOS

This platform powers the ever popular iPhone and iPad. The iPhone ushered in the current generation of smartphones that provide touch screen interfaces, high quality screens and graphics, and an abundance of apps. Although the Android platform has the largest overall market share, the iPhone has the distinction of being the most popular single device.

The key benefits of the iPhone are its ease of use, single vendor solution providing greater consistency and quality control, and apps that are compatible with the iPad. The sales of iPhones and iPads are feeding off each other because of the ability to use a single interface for both devices. On the negative side, the iPhone is still constrained to operating on the slower 3G cellular networks, and it relies on the iTunes application to manage the content. However, this will be eliminated with the new iCloud remote storage service from Apple for the iPhone and iPad. The iPhone only offers a virtual keyboard, which some people find cumbersome to use.

BlackBerry®

It was not that long ago that the BlackBerry devices dominated the market. They were traditionally the best at facilitating e-mail communications, which is what business professionals primarily relied on these devices for. But that all changed with the introduction of the iPhone and then the Android platform. BlackBerry has been a victim of rapidly evolving smartphone technology. Apps replaced e-mail as the most important feature of smartphones in the consumer market, and the consumer market is now driving the business market in these devices.

The BlackBerry does provide the greatest control over managing and configuring multiple devices, which makes it very desirable for mass deployment at the corporate level. It also offers the most options to secure the device and the data stored on it.

Windows Mobile

Microsoft has a lot of ground to make up to be more competitive with the other three platforms, and they are trying. The challenge is that there is not really a market for Windows apps. Apple and Android dominate in this category. The primary opportunity for Microsoft is to design a device that fully exploits the MS Office applications because these are applications that most business professionals use daily to process and exchange business information. Windows Mobile will need to be reassessed after Windows 8 is released.

We have covered a lot of territory in this chapter, but that is because we think it is extremely important to outfit yourself and your staff with the proper software and equipment that will allow you to stay focused on delivering your client services and not be at the mercy of technology. As you transition your infrastructure and applications to the cloud, the toolkit becomes the only substantial piece of your IT model that you need to attend to directly. For those of you who are sole practitioners, the toolkit will be the bulk of your entire IT system, so do not take these recommendations casually. The return on investment will be swift and substantial.

Chapter 6

Scanning Solutions

We start this chapter by clarifying the role of your scanning process, which is to convert paper documents into electronic images that can also be converted into "machine readable" content that can be processed by software applications. This may be as simple as being able to search for specific text in the document or going all the way to recognizing data on a form and transferring that data directly into a software application. A classic example is to identify the wages and compensation figure on a W-2 form and transfer that number directly to the tax preparation software "hands free."

The key topics we will cover in this chapter include the following:

- Centralized versus distributed scanning model
- Alternative scanning devices
- Image processing software
- Document processing software
- Workflow integration

Centralized Versus Distributed Scanning

It is much easier to start a good habit than it is to break a bad habit. The same can be said for defining a business process. It is much easier to design the optimal process from the start, rather than trying to change an ill-conceived process down the road. When it comes to your scanning process, for most of us, it is still early enough in the game to change your approach without disrupting your firm too much. This all relates to choosing the optimal scanning model for your firm: centralized or distributed.

Centralized scanning refers to a model whereby you have only designated people responsible for doing virtually all the firm's scanning at a centralized scanning workstation. *Distributed scanning* refers to having multiple scanning devices located throughout the office, perhaps even at everyone's desk, and everyone is responsible for scanning their own documents. In our opinion, centralized scanning is the better model for a number of reasons, including investing in higher quality scanning equipment and software, having trained scanning operators applying consistent quality control procedures, and implementing a lower cost scanning process through the use of administrative staff to perform an administrative task.

The temptation to use a distributed scanning model exists primarily because people like to have as much control over their workflow as possible. However, this is a case in which failing to relinquish this task to dedicated administrative staff results in inconsistency of quality control and a high cost of labor to scan documents. We suggest that you start showing the time spent scanning on your client invoices at the typical staff rates and see how long it takes for you to get a call from the client. The only legitimate argument for distributed scanning is perhaps to control access to sensitive documents or to expedite scanning of individual documents on demand. To that point, it makes sense to deploy a hybrid model that relies primarily on a centralized scanning operation but also accommodates minimal personal scanning through the distribution of personal scanners throughout the office. However, the more you make the personal scanners available, the more tempting it will be for your professional staff to do all of their own scanning under the misconception that it is more efficient. Box 6-1 outlines the differences between centralized and distributed scanning processes.

Box 6-1: *Centralized vs. Distributed Scanning Models*

Centralized Scanning	Distributed Scanning
Invest in higher quality, higher performance scanners	Invest in multiple lower cost, lower speed, lower quality scanners
Scanning performed by less costly administrative staff	Scanning performed by higher cost professional staff
Invest in high quality image processing software	Invest in multiple copies of high quality image processing software or forgo the benefit
Dedicate a PC for image processing	Utilize multiple PCs for image processing
Establish a consistent quality control model	Inconsistent quality control model varies with each individual

Alternative Scanning Devices

When it comes to procuring your physical scanning devices, you have a wide array of options to choose from. There are four basic form factors to choose from: multifunction printer/scanners (MFPs), Sheet Fed Scanners, Flatbed Scanners, and Portable Scanners.

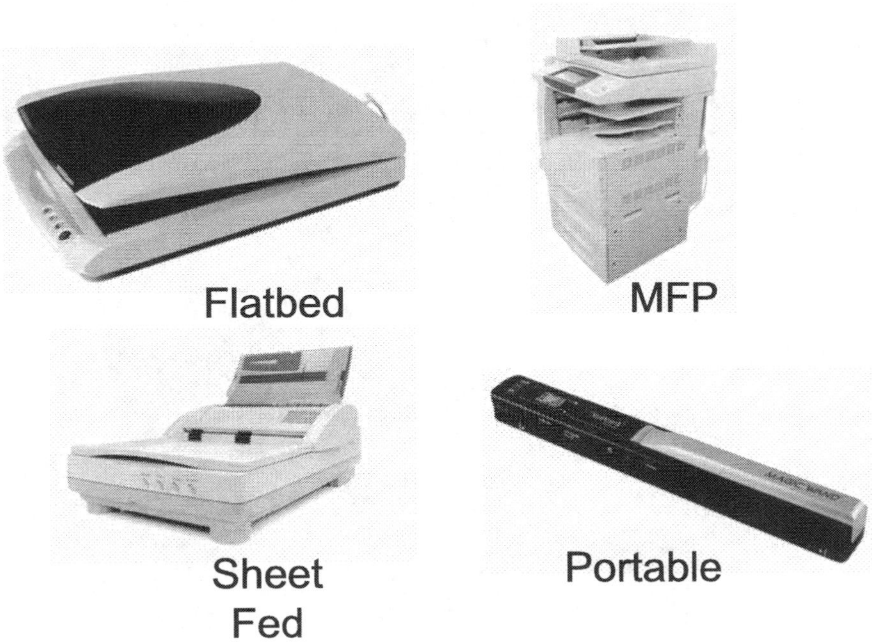

The tables below outline some of the pros and cons of each device to help you determine which has the features that best meet your needs.

Multifunction Printer/Scanners (MFPs)

Pros	Cons
Leverage investment by extending functionality of the copier printer	No option to put on desktop
	Multisheet feeder quality varies
	Large footprint

Sheet Fed Scanners

Pros	Cons
Faster scanning of multipage documents	More moving parts to replace or repair
Smaller footprint	
Direct connect to PC workstation	

Flatbed Scanners

Pros	Cons
Can handle small and large paper sizes	Excessive paper handling with single sheet feeding operation
Fewer moving parts to maintain or repair	Large footprint
Good for scanning book and magazine pages	

Portable Scanners

Source: Used with permission from VuPoint. All product names, logos, brands, and other trademarks referred herein are the property of their respective owners and are used only to describe the product(s) shown in the image.

Pros	Cons
Lightweight and portable	Single sheet feeder bin
Inexpensive	Slow

Do not forget about using your smartphone, tablet, or digital camera as an option for doing single page scanning. These devices are suitable for one-up scanning when you are away from the office or have a document that is too small to feed into your scanner, for example, small cash register receipts.

Scanner Features

Regardless of the form factor you select for your scanner, the key features you want to evaluate include the following:

- **Scanner Speed.** Scanner speed is rated in terms of pages per minute (ppm). Portable scanners typically scan in the range of 5–20 ppm, Sheetfed and multifunction printers (MFP) and scanners 20–100 ppm. Keep in mind that overall performance is also affected by the speed of the document feeder, connection type, and image processing software.
- **Automatic Document Feeder.** The automatic document feeder (ADF) is the tray that holds the stack of documents to be scanned. Obviously, the higher your scanning volume, the larger the capacity that is required. The specific attributes that you want to focus on are the ADF speed, the capacity, and paper handling features, particularly the ability to handle multisized documents.
- **Connectivity.** The type of connection between the scanner and the computer is important because of the impact on overall scanning speed. The USB connection is, by far, the most popular with today's scanners, with lots of flexibility to connect to various types of computers. The SCSI interface is appropriate for dedicated scanning stations that have the scanner connected directly to the PC that will be processing the images in a production environment. MFP devices will typically utilize an ethernet connection like other network attached peripherals.
- **Twain Compliant.** This is an acronym that translates into either "technology without an interesting name" or "never the twain shall meet," depending on whom you ask. Regardless, the nature of a twain compliant scanner is that it allows you to control the scanner device from within your various software applications. For example, you can control the scanner settings from within Adobe Acrobat if it is twain compliant. Otherwise, you will have to process your scanning jobs from the application software provided with the scanner. The good news is that the overwhelming majority of scanners on the market are twain compliant.
- **Image Processing Software.** This is arguably as important as the scanning device itself. Image processing software takes the original document image created by the scanner and cleans it up. The typical features include despeckling to remove stray marks, deskewing to align the document image, blank page recognition and deletion, optical character recognition to convert the image into machine readable text, and image cropping to meet the size of the original document. The most widely used image processing software on the market is Kofax VRS (see appendix C, "Resource Center") and is often included as part of the scanner bundle.

Advanced Document Processing Software for Tax Preparation

There is a niche category of software applications designed specifically to automate the process of scanning and organizing the supporting documents for 1040 tax preparation. The typical set of features these applications offer include the following:

- **Document recognition.** Identifies the type of document for purposes of sorting and bookmarking.
- **Automatic bookmarking**. Generates a bookmark in the PDF file that contains the document name, for example, W2 – General Motors.
- **Document sorting**. Rearranges the scanned image pages into the sequence in which the tax return is typically prepared, that is, W-2s, 1099 INT, 1099 DIV, and so forth.
- **Scraping**. This refers to the process of actually identifying information located on a scanned image and transferring it to a software application. An example of this is scanning a W-2 form and transferring the wages and compensation figure over to the tax preparation software.

An example of these types of software is depicted as figure 6-1.

Figure 6-1: *Sample of GruntWorx 1040 PDF Organizer*

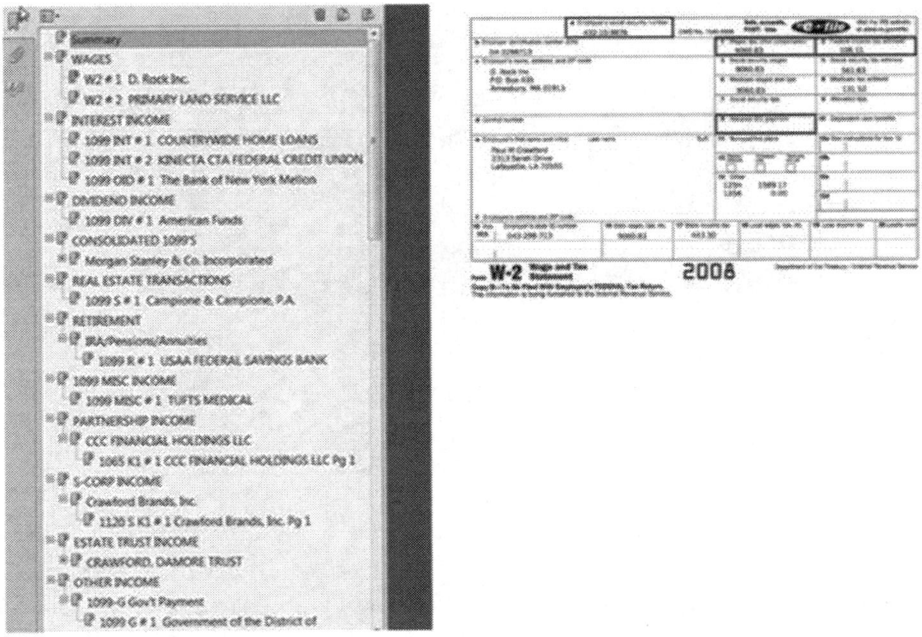

Source: Used with permission from GruntWorx.

Workflow Integration

The most important decision about your scanning system is determining how you will integrate scanning into your core business processes. The key decisions are who will do the scanning and when will it be done. We have already discussed the benefits of centralized scanning versus distributed scanning, so that should make the decision about "who" a little easier.

Deciding when to do your scanning requires analysis of each workflow process and determining what format you want your documents to be in at various stages in the process, that is, paper or electronic image. There are three basic options available to you for every business process: front end, mid-point, and back end scanning.

Front End Scanning

Front end scanning means that you scan all your paper documents before you begin your process, whether it is preparing a tax return, performing an audit test, or compiling a financial statement. If you scan them at the beginning, you then have the ability to establish a truly paperless workflow. Figure 6-2 outlines the front end scanning process.

Figure 6-2: *Front End Scanning = Paperless Workflow*

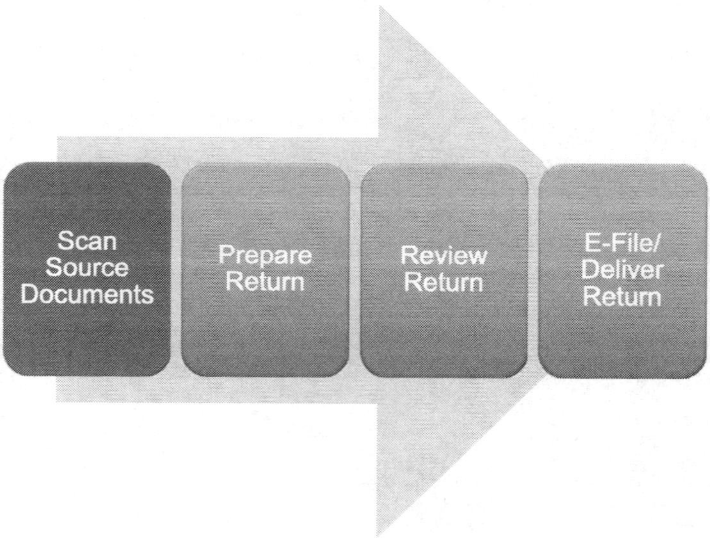

One of the key items to consider with this approach includes deciding where the documents will be stored, so that they can be easily accessed during the process. This is where the document management system plays an important role. You also have to determine how you will annotate your electronic documents with notes and tick marks. This is extremely important because it is the biggest challenge of going paperless, and we will discuss this more fully in the next chapter. Finally, you have to decide what to do with the original paper documents: return them to the client, destroy them, or have them flow through the process using traditional red rope folders. The latter is not recommended because people will be tempted to work with the paper documents instead of the document images, and you will lose the benefit of working with the files in a digital format. You also run the risk of having two sets of documents with different content based on who is working with the online documents versus those who are working with the paper documents. If you are going to keep the original paper documents, our recommendation is to put them in temporary storage during the process if your intent is to return them to the client or destroy them at the end of the process.

Mid-Point Scanning

Mid-point scanning refers to the concept of working with the original paper documents as your working papers for the first part of the process, for example, preparing the return, and then scanning the source documents in at a designated step in the process to convert to working in paperless mode. This might be at a point after the preparation step and before the review process. The optimal point to scan will be different for every process. Figure 6-3 outlines the midpoint scanning process.

Figure 6-3: *Mid-Point Scanning = Hybrid Workflow*

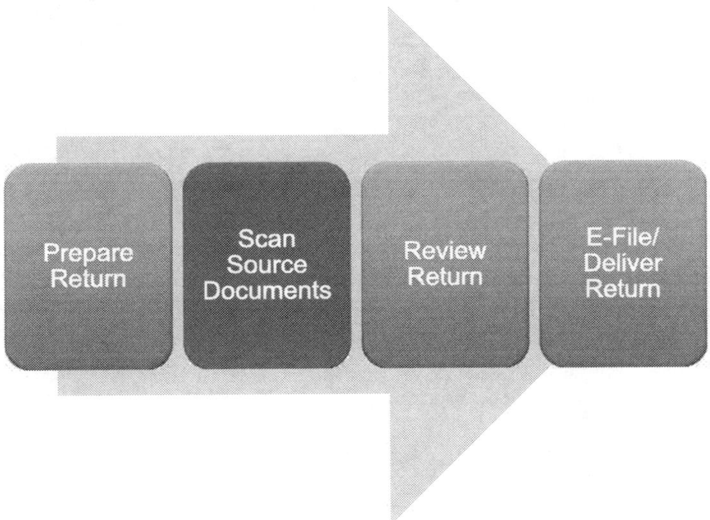

Back End Scanning

Back end scanning is the easiest approach and a good way to get exposure to the whole concept of going paperless. *Back end* scanning refers to working with the documents in paper form throughout the process and then scanning them at the end of the engagement.

The benefit of this approach is that you utilize electronic archiving as opposed to costly and inefficient paper file storage. In addition, you will have your prior year working papers in digital format when the engagement rolls around next year. Figure 6-4 outlines the back end scanning process.

Figure 6-4: *Back End Scanning = Paperless Archiving Only*

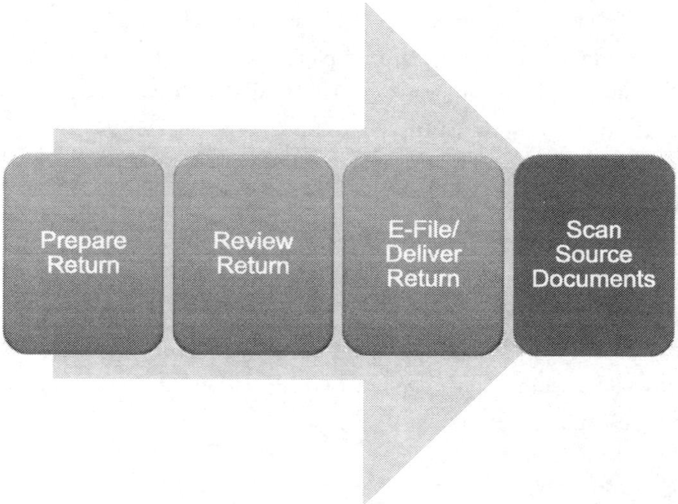

Chapter 7

Document and File Management Systems

The term *document management system*, or DMS, is actually a misnomer. The current generation of DMS software should actually be called *file management systems* because their primary purpose is to provide a more effective solution for managing all your electronic files, compared to using the traditional Windows Explorer folder system. With the exponential growth in the amount of files we are storing due to scanning and e-mail attachments, the inherent deficiencies in the Windows Explorer model are being exposed.

The first generation of DMSs from 20 plus years ago were designed primarily for the purpose of scanning paper documents and managing the storage of the document image files, which were typically stored in tagged image file format or TIFF. Today's DMS systems are designed to manage virtually any type of file and have a much broader scope of features and functions.

From a business process perspective, the key benefit of a DMS is to allow you to access, process, and distribute files more efficiently and to provide controls that are simply not possible in the world of paper documents. The nature of how each DMS handles these functions can be quite different, so you should investigate a number of alternative solutions to gain a better understanding of the whole concept.

Metadata 101

Metadata is defined as "data about data." The metadata is, in essence, separate from the actual data but directly associated with it. We think one of the best (and earliest) examples of metadata is the card catalog system of the public library. You have various types of metadata to help you determine the physical location of a book, such as title, subject, author, and Dewey Decimal number. Any of these metadata values can be used to locate the book. Another example of metadata is the UPC bar code symbol on items at the grocery store. This code is a link to an entire database of information about an item, such as ingredients, pricing information, inventory levels, nutritional information, and so forth.

Figure 7-1: *Acct 1st DMS Metadata Panel*

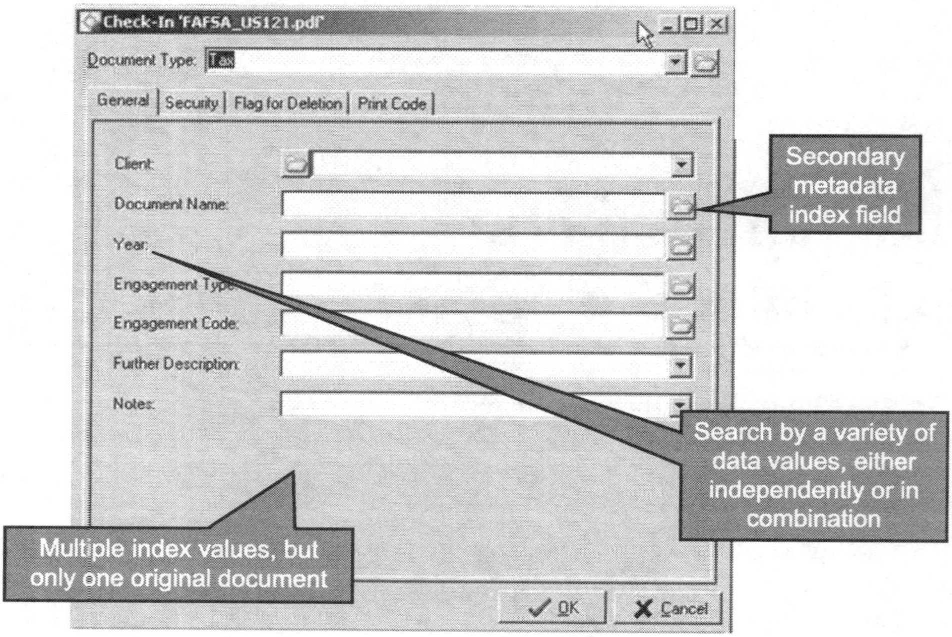

Source: Used with permission from Acct1st Technology Group, LLC.

The same concept applies to locating a document or file in the DMS. You assign metadata values (called *schema*) to your documents. An example of this would include client number, document category, and engagement number. See figure 7-1 for a sample of a metadata entry panel. The key is to find a system that has the flexibility to organize your files by methods that allow you to locate them quickly and logically. The big advantage of metadata is the ability to take different paths to locate the file, just like the book in the library. Compare this to Windows Explorer, which only allows you to access files linearly by navigating through a series of folders and subfolders. Not only are the paths to files getting longer and longer, you are also limited to seeing a list of files located in one folder at a time, for example, 2011 tax returns. With metadata, you can navigate to a list of tax return files that span multiple years with a single search.

Figure 7-2 depicts the four key feature sets of the DMS that you need to evaluate when researching alternative vendor solutions.

Figure 7-2: *Four Key Feature Sets of a DMS*

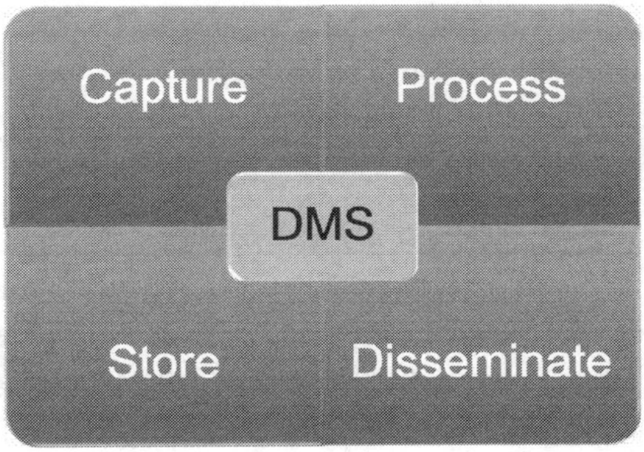

Capture

This refers to the functionality that helps you get documents and files into the DMS initially. The following are the primary methods of input:

- **Scanning and Uploading.** The key feature to look for here is the ability to enter the metadata values at the time of scanning, so that the scanned image can be uploaded to the DMS immediately upon scanning. *Barcoding* the metadata is a feature that allows you to separate the tagging process from the scanning process by using a barcode that links to the metadata. See figure 7-3 for an example of converting metadata to a barcode. The benefit of this process is that your professional staff can perform the initial organization of the documents to be scanned. This feature facilitates the centralized scanning process we discussed in the previous chapter.

Figure 7-3: *Thomson Reuters GoFileRoom DMS Bar Coding Process*

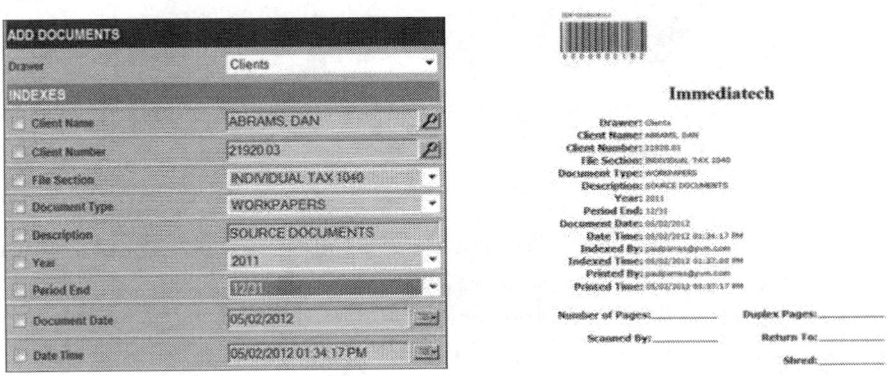

Source: Used with permission from the Tax & Accounting business of Thomson Reuters.

- **Importing E-mail Messages and Attachments.** It seems indisputable that e-mail has become the primary method for exchanging business documents, far surpassing faxes and the postal system. Therefore, a critical feature to evaluate when selecting a DMS is the process for moving e-mail messages and, more importantly, the file attachments, into the DMS and assigning the metadata. You need to see this process demonstrated to properly evaluate the functionality.
- **Publishing Documents and Reports to DMS.** In terms of workflow efficiency, you can eliminate some unnecessary steps in your processes if you focus on publishing your documents and reports in electronic format from the original source directly into the DMS. For example, a final tax return can be printed directly to PDF format and saved into the DMS directly by using information from the source application to populate the metadata automatically. The tax software has the client name, type of return, preparer, date prepared, and fiscal year. All these data elements can be useful as metadata. This is a feature that typically puts the software suite vendors at a competitive advantage because they can build this integration in behind the scenes.
- **Save to DMS.** Keep in mind that a key objective of the DMS is to eliminate your reliance on Windows Explorer as much as possible for storing and retrieving your data files and electronic documents. The closer you get to achieving this goal, the greater your return on investment in the DMS. In order to achieve this goal, you want the process of saving files to the DMS to be at least as easy as storing it to Windows Explorer. This is much easier said than done. If storing is more cumbersome than using the "File Save As" command, then your staff will push back on the use of the system, especially because they are so accustomed to working with Windows Explorer. Keep in mind the primary value of using metadata is on the search and retrieval side of the process, so a certain level of effort on the storage side can be justified on that basis. You should evaluate all your core software applications to determine how a particular DMS will facilitate the storage and retrieval of documents and files. Ideally, the DMS will feature the use of metadata templates to help streamline the indexing and storing of common documents, for example, 1040 documents.

Process

This is the second of our four primary DMS features to evaluate and refers to the tools that facilitate working with documents that are stored in the system. Specifically, you should look for the following capabilities:

- Embedded annotation tools for notes, stamps, markups, redaction, and so forth. The alternative is to use Adobe Acrobat, which is a reasonable option.
- Version control to facilitate storing the various iterations of a document throughout its life cycle.
- Check-out and check-in controls to ensure that only one person is editing the document at a time, while allowing others to view the current copy of the document online.

- Workflow automation features to manage the flow of the documents through the engagement process. See chapter 10, "Workflow Software."

Store

This functionality addresses the tools that are provided to help you manage the file through its life cycle including the following:

- **Access Permissions.** There are two key permission control categories to evaluate. The first is related to controlling who can access files. Ideally, this can be controlled at the user level individually or by role, client or client type, document or document type, and document status. The second level of permission relates to what the user can do with the document (view, print, edit, export, e-mail, delete, and so forth).
- **Retention Management.** Many DMSs have built-in automated retention management that will facilitate the purging of documents when they achieve their expiration date. This is typically addressed by associating a retention period with the type of document, for example, tax documents = 7-year life cycle.
- **Activity Logging.** Ideally, the DMS will maintain a detailed log of all the activity associated with a document that includes who, what, and when for uploading, editing, printing, e-mailing, and so forth.
- **Encryption.** It is always a best practice to have your data stored in encrypted format. The specific method for encryption does not matter particularly; it could be handled within the DMS, your operating system, or some other utility. Refer to our discussion of encryption in chapter 12 for more information on this topic.
- **Anytime, Anywhere Access.** We identified this as a key overall objective of the digital practice model. The easiest way to achieve this is through a secure cloud-based solution. There are many vendors who offer this option, either through a SaaS or hosting model option as described in chapter 3, "Infrastructure." The DMS is one of the most important applications to provide this level of access because there are many situations when staff are in the field and want to access documents. Or perhaps you are having lunch with a client and you want to review a document on your iPad.

Disseminate

Last, but not least, we want to address the options available for distributing your documents to clients and various third parties in a secure format. The following is a list of the more common ways you want to be able to distribute your documents from your DMS:

- **E-Mail.** Again, this is the most frequently used method for sharing documents today, so you need to evaluate how efficient it is to send a file via e-mail attachment directly from the DMS. Specific features to look for include selecting and zipping multiple documents together, password access and encryption, and sending as a link rather than as an attachment.

- **Portal.** This is rapidly becoming a preferred alternative to e-mail. This refers to providing clients and others with a login to a secure section of your website that gives them exclusive access to specified documents and files that they can view, print, or download. The key here is to look for a DMS that has an integrated portal, which will streamline the process of publishing and removing files from the portal. If it is not an integrated portal, the amount of labor involved to manage the content increases significantly, as well as the potential to post the files to the wrong client.
- **Fax.** This is becoming much less important because most people prefer to receive documents via e-mail rather than as a fax. However, to the extent that there are situations when faxing is the preferred option, it is helpful to be able to fax directly from the DMS through an online faxing system such as eFax (www.efax.com). The process of printing and then faxing through a traditional fax machine should be eliminated from all of your processes. The online faxing model is cheaper, more secure, and more efficient.
- **Print.** No matter how committed you are to going paperless, there will be times when you simply need to generate a printed copy of a document directly out of the DMS.
- **Export.** This refers to making a copy of the document or file for storage outside the DMS. There are many situations when this may be necessary. Perhaps you want to move a document to your iPad or laptop for remote offline access or transfer it to a USB drive to deliver to someone in electronic format. If you do not have the option to e-mail a file directly out of your DMS (which should be a mandatory feature), then you will have no option but to export and then e-mail the file as an attachment outside the DMS.

If you focus on the preceding features we just described, you will be much more likely to procure a DMS that will be easier to integrate into your workflows and convert to paperless processes. We cannot overemphasize the importance of participating in a thorough demonstration of the system before you purchase it from the vendor. It is very important to see how the specific features and functions work, rather than just review a list of them provided by the vendor. Fortunately, all the vendors can provide you with a full demo via the Internet, so you never need to leave your office to do your research and evaluation.

The Big Picture

It is important to understand that the DMS is at the core of your paperless practice model. It is the hub into and out of which all your electronic documents will flow. For that reason, it is not an easy application to deploy and requires a great deal of forethought and evaluation. Integration with your other core applications is critical to your ability to truly automate your processes and leverage the full benefit of digital documents. This is illustrated in the following figure 7-4.

Figure 7-4: *Integration of DMS With Other Core Applications*

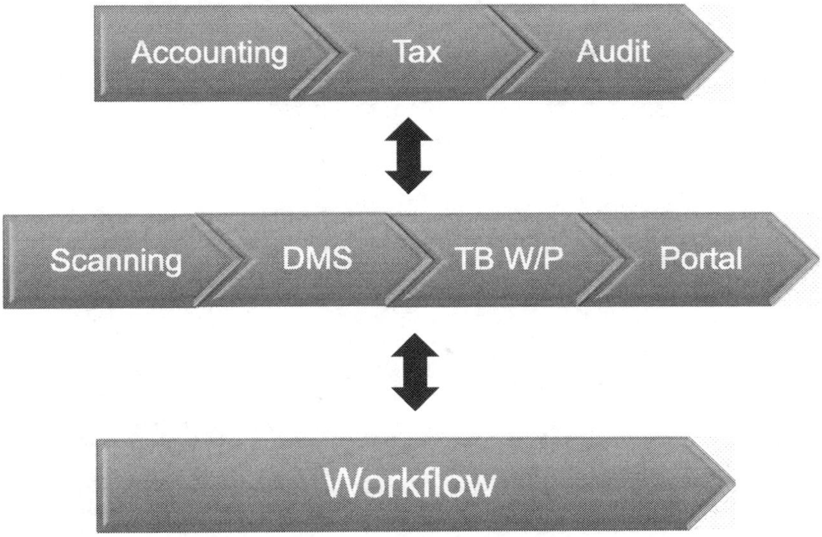

DMS Implementation Best Practices

There are a lot of things to consider when deploying a DMS, and it is easy to shortcut the process. Based on our experience in helping over 100 firms implement a DMS and the related applications, it is clear that investing in the research of the optimal solution for your firm and planning how you will integrate the DMS into your workflows pays big dividends.

Table 7-1 is a list of best practices for optimizing the implementation of a DMS in your practice. Many of these apply to other software applications as well but are of particular importance for the DMS implementation.

Table 7-1: *DMS Implementation Best Practices*

Analyze and document processes to define how the DMS will be integrated into your workflows
Focus on moving from back end scanning to front end scanning model for process optimization
Utilize bar coding to separate metadata assignment from the scanning process
Establish a policy for what types of e-mails get moved into the DMS
Develop a plan for integration with workflow and portal applications
Map out metadata tagging model for all key document types in advance of deployment
Establish a deadline for turning off access to public server folders for document storage
Conduct a pilot program to process a prior year engagement through the DMS and related applications prior to deployment
Document key policies and procedures
Develop a training program that includes software usage and business process

Chapter 8

Trial Balance Working Paper Software

We made a few assumptions when writing this book, and one of them is that you already have your tax preparation software, so we do not need to spend time discussing it here. In a certain sense, we made the same assumption regarding trial balance software. However, we wanted to be sure to cover the niche category of trial balance software that is used to manage the working paper files related to trial balance based engagements, that is, compilations, reviews, audits, and entity tax returns. There is not really a clearly defined name for this category of software, so we are going to use the term *trial balance working paper* software. We are covering this topic on the heels of the document management system (DMS) software discussion because you can make a credible argument that this is a form of document management software.

We will begin by explaining the nature of trial balance working paper software. The primary function is to serve as a trial balance software application with direct links to all the supporting digital working paper files, as well as to link directly into a financial statement reporting application and to transfer the trial balance data directly into the tax software. This application can be one of the most challenging to implement successfully because it requires you to redesign your workflows to be compatible with the design of the software. This is a good thing but can mean a lot of that ugly thing we call "change." Although it may be a challenge to successfully deploy, on the flip side, it can be one of the best technology investments you can make because it has the potential to drive out several inefficiencies in your trial balance engagement processes. Firms that have committed to fully implement this software have reported reductions of more than 30 percent in the time it takes to complete a full engagement cycle. That is substantial! Unfortunately, our experience has been that many firms struggle to fully implement the software as it was intended to be used and, therefore, end up with a hybrid approach that results in little or no efficiency gains. So the point you should take away from this is if you are going to make the investment, then you need to make the commitment to fully implement it.

Figure 8-1: *Trial Balance Working Paper Software Features*

Features Review

Let's examine each of the components of this software (as shown in preceding figure 8-1) so that you will have a better appreciation for all that it can do for your firm. We describe each component in a generic sense. The actual approach to how each piece is implemented is what differentiates one vendor's solution from another. That is why you need to do your research.

Trial Balance

This is the core feature of the application. It is a fairly typical trial balance (TB) application that reports on the TB from the unadjusted state to the adjusted TB, with columns to track the various journal entries. The TB is typically presented in a spreadsheet-like format with the option to view it in the various iterations, for example, tax basis, cash basis, and so forth. In fact, the TB component may be presented in an Excel worksheet format.

Journal Entries

This is the functionality that lets you record your various journal entries, such as adjusting, reclassifying, tax, cash basis, and so forth. In addition to having the ability to record extended explanations, there may be the ability to track approval and submission of all the entries. There will definitely be a link to the supporting working paper file or lead sheet, or both, whereby a journal entry impact will be presented on the working paper.

Financial Statements

There will be a direct link from the trial balance to the financial statement reporting tool. The obvious benefit is that whenever a change is made to the TB it is directly reflected in the financial statements. The key feature here is the ability to format the financial statements with as much flexibility as possible to meet your firm's reporting style, while at the same time providing the appropriate level of structure to incorporate various checks and balances. Typical features include the ability to group accounts into a line item, create supporting detail schedules, full footnote disclosure, and the accountant's letter. Some programs utilize Excel or Word as the financial reporting application with the appropriate links to the TB.

Working Paper Binder

This is the feature that really distinguishes this application from typical TB software—the ability to have a structured repository for all the files that support the TB, such as PDF files, e-mail messages, data files, Excel spreadsheets, Word documents, and so forth. The binder will include a referencing system to associate the working paper document with the appropriate accounts in the TB. This is where it can start to get a little fuzzy in terms of the relationship to the DMS. Many of these systems were designed before document management came onto the tax and accounting software scene. Therefore, there originally was no integration between the two applications. However, as the DMS and working paper software applications continue to evolve, we are starting to see a move toward leveraging the DMS as the working paper binder rather than having it as a stand-alone application.

Engagement Management

Another aspect of these engagements that complicates the application is that many trial balance engagements, particularly reviews and audits, are completed by a team working collaboratively on the engagement simultaneously. Therefore, the whole process of managing the access to working papers for editing and review is an important component. The check-out/check in features play an important role in controlling changes to the working papers. You will want to understand how this process works in each solution you evaluate.

Additional engagement management features include a structured working paper sign-off process that tracks preparer completion, reviewer approval, and so forth. The ability to lock down the working paper file at the completion of the engagement is also important in order to comply with the appropriate auditing standards.

Review Notes

This feature could have been discussed previously with the other engagement management features, but we feel it is important enough to stand on its own. One of the biggest challenges in moving to paperless workflows in a CPA firm is automating the working paper review process, as we discussed in the previous chapter. We do not need to cover that ground again here, but what you want to evaluate in a working paper system is the entire review note tracking and management process. Some of the specific features to focus on include categorizing review notes by type; stamping the date, time, and author; locking the note from edits; linking the note to a working paper or TB line item, or both; and the ability to purge selected notes and integration with e-mail to facilitate review note processing.

Tax Software Bridge

This is a very important feature for entity tax engagements because of the opportunity to streamline the process of moving the trial balance data directly into the tax software hands free. If you think this whole process through, you will realize that once you record a journal entry in the TB, the impact will flow directly to the financial statements, supporting schedules, tax return, and appropriate working papers. That is when you begin to realize the full potential of this application to streamline your workflows.

Accounting Software Bridge

This is a client side feature in that it allows you to import your client's unadjusted trial balance data from his or her accounting system directly into the TB. The obvious benefit is another example of the hands-free transfer of data from one system to the next. Remember our discussion about the pyramid in chapter 1, "The Nature of the Digital Practice Model and the Benefits to You and Your Firm"? The key feature to look for here is to make sure the import function is compatible with the various accounting systems that your clients are using. This is actually less important than it used to be simply because most modern day accounting systems have the ability to export directly to a standard Excel file format or a comma separated values format. Either of these file formats can be imported by all the leading TB working paper software applications. You should also look for preformatted import templates for your client's accounting systems and the ability to build your own templates. This will significantly minimize the time you need to spend completing the import process.

Solutions Overview

The array of software products for this application can be put into two categories: full featured and basic. If your firm has a substantial book of review and audit engagements, then you are most likely going to want to choose from the three market leaders: Caseware, Engagement CS (Thomson Reuters), and ProFx Engagement (CCH). We recommend that you take the time to thoroughly review each of these offerings by participating in a live webinar demonstration. There are distinct differences between them. If your practice is limited primarily to compilations and entity tax returns, you may be better advised to go with a simpler TB program that doesn't have the depth of features as those listed previously. You don't need to be constrained by the necessary structure those more sophisticated programs offer for a team approach to engagements. A simple TB program, such as Accountants World and many others in that market, will likely suit your needs.

There is one last point we would like to make on this topic. Due to the nature of the design of these programs to be used in a collaborative environment, with features like checking files in and out to support a mix of field work and in-firm activities, they need to have sophisticated features to facilitate and manage the distribution and collection of working paper files. As a result, there are more issues related to moving these applications to the cloud. Therefore, they are one of the last applications that we see being redeployed as cloud-based solutions. This is ironic because these applications can probably benefit the most from being deployed through the cloud because of their use in the field. So if you are intent on deploying this application through the cloud, be sure to do the appropriate level of due diligence and evaluate the vendor's track record for leveraging the cloud.

Chapter 9

Client Portals—Gateway to the Future

The topic of portals can be as broad in scope as talking about information technology or the Internet. Let's begin with a baseline definition of a *client portal*, which is a secure link on your website to personalized information and applications. In a broader sense, think of your client portal as the gateway between the world of cloud-based information and applications that your clients use to manage their business and personal financial affairs and the various devices that they use to access that information: desktop computers, laptops, smartphones, and tablets. When you approach your client portal strategy from this perspective, you soon realize the depth of potential to serve your clients better and strengthen their relationship with your firm.

Figure 9-1: *The Client Portal as Gateway*

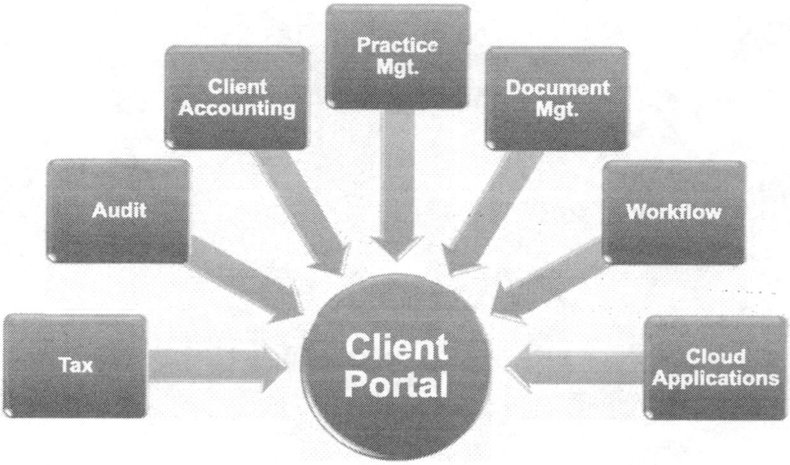

Your client portal should ultimately touch every aspect of your client services, as shown in figure 9-1. It can evolve to serve as a gateway for your clients to all the financial information and applications they need to run their business and personal affairs. In this chapter, we will define the value proposition of the client portal (see figure 9-2) and then provide a process for developing your portal strategy.

Figure 9-2: *The Client Portal Value Proposition*

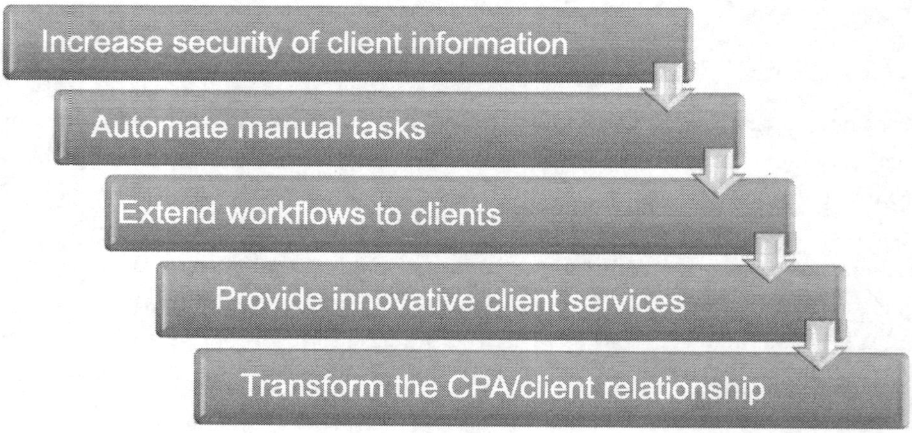

Security

One of the primary forces driving CPA firms to implement a client portal is to reduce the risk of a breach of privacy associated with e-mailing documents that contain personal information, such as tax returns, financial statements, investment information, and so forth. If you deploy an effective portal system, it can be one of the most secure ways to exchange and store information today.

Task Automation

Another key feature of the client portal is to automate otherwise labor intensive tasks related to exchanging documents and other information with your clients. Take the example of transmitting a copy of a client's tax return to him or her. Using the postal system is extremely labor intensive because you have to print the document, create and stuff the envelope, apply postage, and deliver to the post office, where even more labor is involved to transfer it from point A to point B. Even if you are utilizing e-mail, you have to generate a PDF copy of the return, create an e-mail message, and attach the file. With an effective portal solution that is integrated with a document management system which, in turn, is integrated with the tax software, it can be virtually a few clicks of the mouse to publish the tax return to the portal. This is one simple example of an opportunity for the portal to help automate your processes. Of course, the information has to be in digital format in order for all of this to work.

Extended Workflows

The concept of extended workflows means that you provide your clients a better service by offering them the opportunity to have greater access to their information. An abundance of opportunities are available to integrate your clients directly into your workflows by leveraging the cloud. The following are some examples of how you can extend your workflows to your clients:

- Provide updates when the status of their engagement changes.
- Facilitate the opportunity for them to answer engagement-related questions via the portal.
- Give them the ability to enter their organizer data online through the portal.
- Offer online payment of their invoices via credit card.
- Present a preliminary check register or open invoice list for payment approval.
- Present their engagement letter for online review, approval, and signature.
- Incorporate a draft review of reports and tax filings into your workflow.

The opportunities will continue to evolve with the next generation of accounting and tax software and the increased use of cloud-based applications. The beauty of this concept is that it not only enhances the value of your client services, it also has the potential to eliminate some of the steps in your current business processes.

Innovative Services

This is the aspect of client portals that gets us the most excited. There is an unprecedented opportunity to transform the nature of how you service your clients by making your portal their gateway to a virtually unlimited array of financial information and services to help them manage their business and personal affairs. In order to fully appreciate the opportunity, you really have to think outside the box and brainstorm about how you can provide value to your clients through your portal. You may want to invest in a professional facilitator to help you through this process.

The following are just a few examples of ways to provide innovative client services through your portal:

- Schedule automatic e-mail reminders two weeks before tax estimate payments are due that includes the amount and a link back to the portal to download the estimate payment voucher.
- Provide a comprehensive online personal financial plan that compares plan results to actual results in real time via single sign-on to financial accounts (see www.emoney-advisors.com in appendix C, "Resource Center").
- Provide a comprehensive financial and accounting service via the portal using a cloud-based accounting system (see www.intacct.com in appendix C). Use this as the foundation of a multilevel service offering virtual bookkeeper, virtual controller, or virtual CFO services. Each offering would include a progressively broader bundle of tax, accounting, and financial services, with emphasis on delivery through the portal. Refer to chapter 11, "Cloud-Based Client Accounting System" for an expanded discussion of this topic.

The bottom line is that the value proposition for a client portal is substantial and will evolve and grow substantially over the coming years as the transition to cloud computing and the proliferation of mobile devices continue at their rapid pace.

Developing Your Portal Strategy

Due to the long-term potential of the client portal to fundamentally transform the way you communicate and exchange information with your clients, developing a portal strategy is highly recommended. We will provide a roadmap for developing a portal strategy that can be deployed over an extended period of time based on your priorities and resources.

Figure 9-3: *Portal Development Roadmap*

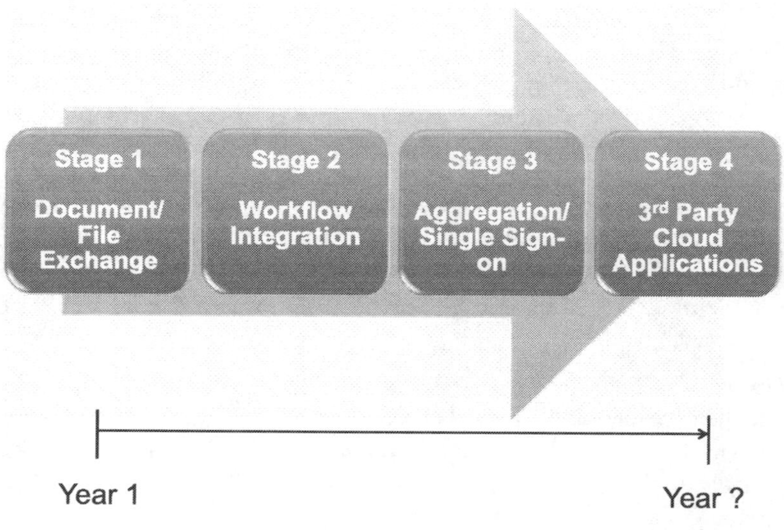

Keep in mind that as we define each stage of your portal development, you are likely to have multiple subportals converge into your primary client portal site. Think about the desktop icons on your PC or iPad that take you to many different applications. The same holds true for your portal. You ultimately want to have a single, secure web page that your client logs into to gain access to all the information and applications that you offer. Do not think of your portal as being limited to one specific vendor solution.

As previously illustrated in figure 9-3, your portal strategy should be defined in stages. You can determine the stages that are most appropriate for your firm. However, we believe that the roadmap provided here is logical and can be implemented according to your timetable. The following text defines each stage in greater detail.

Stage 1: Document and File Exchange

This is, by far, the most prevalent portal model deployed by CPAs today. It is a great place to start because it is relatively easy compared to the other stages, and the benefit will be realized relatively quickly. The objective of this stage is to provide your clients with a convenient and secure solution for storing their information in the cloud so that they can access it anytime, from anywhere, with their PCs, smartphones, and tablets. You also want to provide them the ability to upload documents and files directly to your portal.

The optimal way to deploy this stage of your portal is to have a portal that is directly integrated with your document management system so that files can be published and removed from the portal with minimal effort. Your goal for this stage should be to work toward a model in which every document and file you exchange with your clients flows through the portal. The two key criteria to focus on are security of the portal and the ease of uploading and downloading files on both ends.

The primary value proposition for this stage is based in the reduction in manual effort required to distribute documents and files through the postal system or e-mail and increasing the control over information privacy and providing clients with better, self-service based access to their documents.

You can also leverage this platform to begin offering some innovative client services with relative ease. Why not post a PDF file of all their 1040 source documents that you spent time scanning and organizing into a quality document? Post copies of the tax estimate payment vouchers for each quarter in case they happen to lose the copy you delivered with the tax return. Another innovative service is to offer clients the opportunity to have their personal documents uploaded to the secure portal as a reliable, safety deposit box for birth certificates, insurance policies, mortgage contracts, wills, and so forth. It will not cost much for you but may be perceived as a valuable service by your clients and another opportunity to keep them engaged with your firm via the portal. Figure 9-4 shows types of files that can be shared through the portal.

Figure 9-4: *Document/File Exchange*

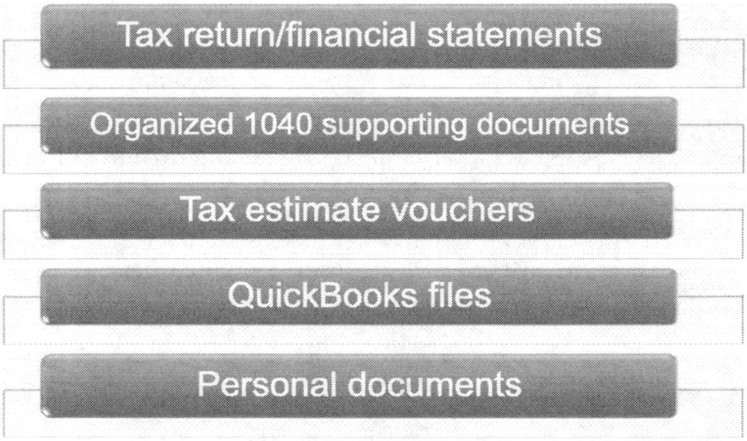

Stage 2: Workflow Integration

Once you have established a reliable portal offering for document and file exchange, a natural progression is to utilize the portal to extend your workflows. The objective here is to further automate your business processes to eliminate manual procedures and provide your clients with more timely and relevant information.

Figure 9-5: *Extending Your Workflows to Clients Via the Portal*

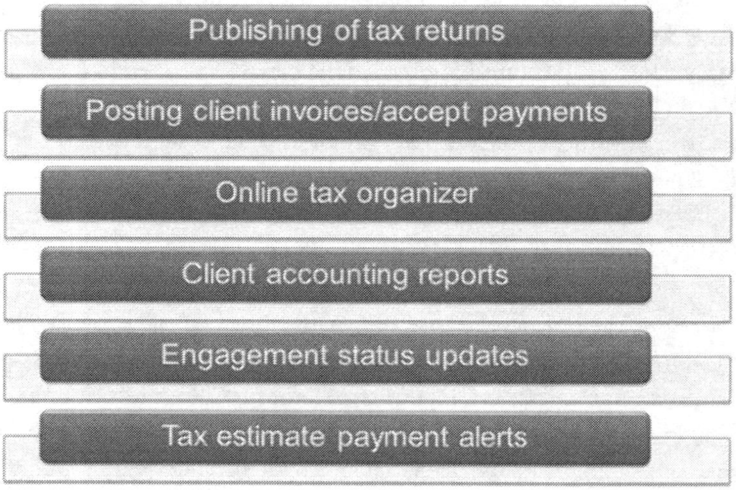

Figure 9-5 illustrates some examples of using the portal for workflow integration. If you have a heavy tax practice, you will want a portal that is directly integrated with the tax software so that the returns can be published directly to the portal in PDF format. Publish client invoices to the portal and send them an e-mail with a link to retrieve it and provide the capability to accept credit card payments. Many clients want the opportunity to pay online, and it will improve your cash flow. If taxi cab drivers can accept electronic payments, then surely CPA firms should be capable of the same. If you have a workflow application, you should be able to include your clients in the process and send them updates on their engagements when they reach key milestones. Our favorite is to set up the portal to send automatic notifications of tax estimates that are due two weeks in advance, with a link to the actual voucher stored on the portal.

If you can implement even a few of these ideas, you will further enhance the relationship between your clients and your firm.

Stage 3: Aggregation and Single Sign-on

This is where your portal starts to get more complex but also much more valuable to your clients. Think about it, everyone these days has multiple websites they log into to view their financial information, such as bank accounts, insurance accounts, brokerage accounts, and so forth. If you can setup your portal to provide a single point of access for your clients that provides them with a view of all their financial information, your portal will become a financial lifeline for your clients that they will visit on a regular basis and associate your firm as the primary caretaker of all their financial affairs. Figure 9-6 shows some examples of applications that can be provided with a single sign-on.

Figure 9-6: *Provide Single Sign-on Via Your Portal*

Stage 4: Third Party Cloud Applications

If you are familiar with Maslow's hierarchy of needs theory, you will recall that he described the achievement of self-actualization as the pinnacle of success in fulfilling one's needs. In portal terms, stage four is the equivalent of self-actualization. The concept here is to embed access to key software applications that your clients need to manage their business and personal financial affairs. Just like you, they will also be trying to figure out how to leverage the cloud and make the transition. You can make this process much easier for them by serving as their trusted source for these applications.

Figure 9-7: *Third Party Cloud Applications*

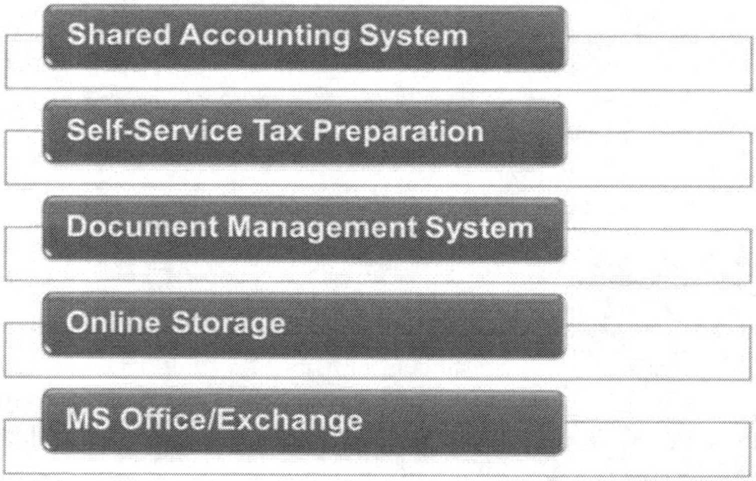

Think back to the 1990s when many CPA firms attempted to enter into the IT services market. Many attempted to sell accounting software, and a smaller number actually sold computer equipment and networking systems. The results overall were pretty dismal; only a relatively small percentage of firms were successful in IT services. Most firms failed for a number of reasons, not the least of which was their lack of expertise in this area. Contributing to the problem was the fact that accounting software, at that time, was buggy, complex, and overkill for what most small businesses were prepared to deal with. Then, out of nowhere, came QuickBooks, which was an instant success because of its simplicity and low cost.

The point we want to make here is that with cloud computing and the maturity of the accounting software market, the opportunity to deliver your clients an innovative accounting solution through your portal is unprecedented. This provides an opportunity to clearly differentiate your firm. Not only will this enhance your value to your clients, it will also help you transform your portal into a profit center that is based primarily on technology, rather than labor. You can also deliver many other practical business applications to your clients through your portal, such as MS Exchange, QuickBooks, MS Office, document management, and so forth, as shown in figure 9-7. It's a great time to consider moving your firm back into IT services via the cloud. The key difference today is that you only have to deal with a relatively miniscule amount of core technology issues and security because that will all be handled by the application provider. That is why it is called "software as a service."

Portal Deployment Checklist

We strongly encourage you to invest some time in developing your long-term portal strategy before you get too far down the path with stage one. The following is an outline for a process to develop your strategy and roll out your portal.

Portal Deployment Checklist

1. **Establish a portal team and assign a champion.** You should ensure that there is representation from each of your service lines, including firm administration, to make sure all areas of the firm are represented. You may want to consider your firm administrator as the champion for this initiative because he or she will have a bird's eye view of the entire firm and will be in the best position to work directly with IT to make sure the portal technology is implemented effectively.
2. **Establish your portal goals.** Anytime you can establish realistic goals, the more likely you will be to stay focused and achieve success. Remember, it is always easy to set goals that may be hard to achieve in reality, so do not try to bite off too much too soon. Your portal should start out simple and evolve and expand over time. Some types of goals you may want to set include client usage and activity, specific tasks that will be automated, defining the scope of content, and calculated cost savings.
3. **Define your content strategy.** It is important to develop a plan for what information and services you want to offer through the portal. We believe that the four-stage evolution we have outlined is logical and achievable. It may well take three to five years or more to achieve stage four, so develop a long-term content strategy but focus in detail on stage one and work toward achieving success there before moving on to the other stages. This may be as simple as publishing the last three years of reports you have generated for the client, for example, tax returns, financial statements, payroll reports, and so forth. Be innovative here over the long term.
4. **Research and select your portal technology.** This may be the most difficult part of the entire process. You will need to have a clear understanding of how you want your portal to evolve in the coming years, so you can find a solution that will help you achieve your goals. However, finding a portal solution today that can address your long-term goals and objectives may be too much to take on at one time. As a first step, you may want to focus on a portal solution that can accommodate stage one, as defined previously. This will get you through the next two to three years and will provide time for the market of portal technology to mature further and provide time for your firm to develop a more refined portal strategy for the long term.
5. **Workflow integration.** Once you have selected and implemented your portal solution, take the time to have your team walk through each of your core processes that involve direct exchange of information with your clients, such as tax services, accounting, payroll, and billing. For each process, identify where you are capturing information from clients and where you are distributing information to them. Analyze the opportunity to capture and disseminate this information via the portal instead of the current process, such as the postal system, e-mail, thumb drive, fax, and so forth. As part of this process, try to calculate the potential reduction in labor that will result, as well as any other benefits, so that you can measure the overall value proposition of your portal investment.

6. **Document, pilot, and train.** After you complete step 5, assign responsibility for someone to document the new procedures. This should be done initially at the macro level and then ultimately at the micro level. We are big believers in piloting the deployment of new technology before it is rolled out on a broad basis. This is even more important with the portal because of its direct impact on your clients. The pilot process should consist of the following steps, as shown in table 9-1.

Table 9-1: *Portal Pilot Project Plan*

Portal Pilot Project Plan
1. Identify half a dozen clients that you can invite to be part of the pilot. Be sure they are representative of your core service lines.
2. Reach out to these clients and communicate what you are trying to accomplish, and get their permission to be a part of the pilot. Most clients will appreciate the fact that you have singled them out for this initiative.
3. Gather all the paper and electronic files you have stored for them for the past three to five years. Analyze each document and file and determine if you want to make this available to them over the portal.
4. Walk through the procedures for setting up a client's portal account including login credentials, permission levels, password policy, client authorization, and so forth.
5. Upload all the files and conduct internal tests for logging in and viewing, printing, and downloading files from the portal. Develop user documentation for this process that is simple and very graphic, so that it will be easy for clients to understand. Have one or two of your less technically savvy staff pilot the procedures for logging into the portal to view, print, and download files.
6. Repeat the previous steps for the process of uploading a file to the portal externally, for example, a client's QuickBooks data file.
7. After you have completed your internal testing, schedule a private training session with each of your pilot clients to walk them through the process of accessing the portal to retrieve documents and upload files. Optimally, you should send someone from your office to train them in person. Alternatively, utilize GoToMeeting (www.gotomeeting.com) or some other web conference system to train them online. Anticipate problems and be prepared to address them ASAP so that you can make the experience as positive as possible for the clients.
8. Once you have successfully completed your pilot, execute a roll out plan for the rest of your client base. We recommend that you do this on a phased approach, perhaps 25–50 clients per month, so that you do not overwhelm your staff and are able to respond to client training and support needs.
9. Promote the portal. Do not expect that just because you built it, they will come. You need to establish a complete marketing strategy that includes an e-mail campaign (include in your newsletter if you have one), and train your staff to communicate about the new service to clients when they are in contact with them. The focus should be centered on the benefits to the client: convenience and security.
10. Survey clients after a period of three to six months to determine if they are using the portal, and get their feedback so that you can make adjustments. Do not expect a high rate of activity initially. It will take time, but the usage should grow on a steady basis as long as you keep making your clients aware of the portal service.

This is one of the most important initiatives that firms will be involved with over the next decade. Expect to see a significant increase in the availability of portal tools and applications in the coming years. Do not try to bite off more than you can chew, but do not sit on the sidelines either.

Chapter 10

Workflow Software

Of all the digital practice initiatives we are presenting in this book, workflow software is likely to be the one you are least familiar with. Ironically, this may prove to be one of the most important initiatives because in a certain way, it is the glue that binds all the other initiatives together. We will explain the nature of workflow software and provide guidance about how you can implement it in your practice to manage your paperless business processes.

The origin of workflow software is based in the need to provide a tool to manage the flow of engagements or documents in a paperless environment. Think about how many practitioners manage the flow of their engagements in a traditional model by relying on the use of red rope and Redweld expanding file pockets to store the engagement working papers, including current year, prior, and the permanent file. A typical scenario goes like this: The folders on the floor on the left side of the desk are the clients I am working on next; the folders on the floor to the right of my desk are the ones I am ready to transfer to the next person in line: the folders behind me on the credenza are the ones that I am waiting for information from the client; and the folder on my desk is the client I am currently working on. Does this scenario sound familiar to you? Chances are you have employed some variation of this workflow management in the past. When you go paperless, this method is no longer an option. That is where workflow software comes in.

Figure 10-1 is a screen shot of the XCM (www.xcmsolutions.com) workflow system, which depicts integration with the ProFx Document document management system from CCH (www.cchgroup.com).

Figure 10-1: *XCM Workflow Software With Integration to CCH ProFx Document DMS*

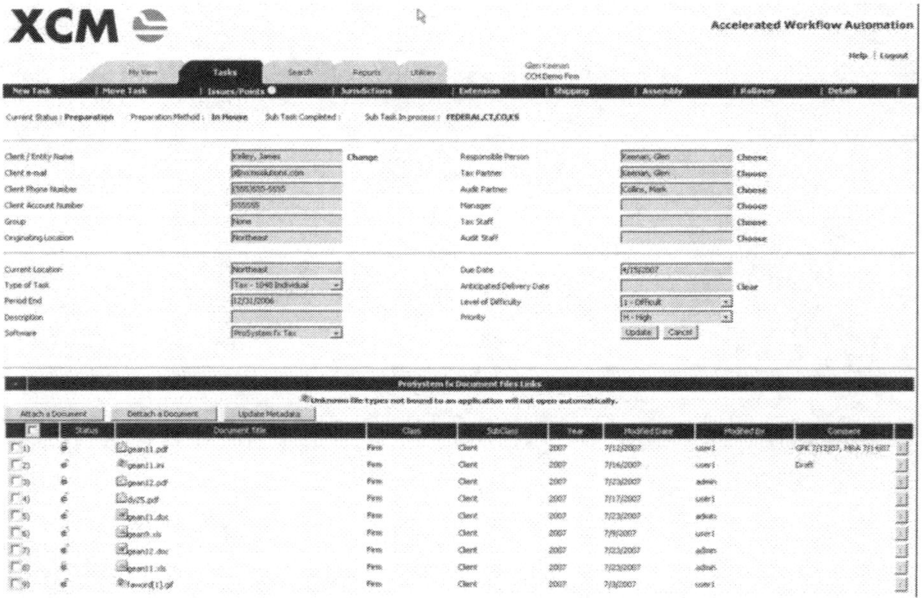

Source: Used with permission from XCM.

The primary role of workflow software is to manage the flow of paperless engagements. However, because the information is all digital, there is so much more that the software can offer. Figure 10-2 is a list of the key features that workflow software typically has to offer.

Figure 10-2: *Key Features of Workflow Software*

Process Mapping

Process mapping entails identifying each of the key steps in a business process that an engagement flows through, for example, tax preparation moves to tax review. Typically, the steps will be when the engagement moves from one person to the next but can be more granular than that, such as when the status changes, like when a tax return is put on extension. As a best practice recommendation, you should start out with very basic steps while your firm is getting accustomed to using the workflow software. Keep it simple.

Scheduling and Task Assignment

This allows you to assign specific staff or skill level groups to perform each step in the process. Some of the more sophisticated workflow systems will integrate this information with a comprehensive staff scheduling module.

Dynamic Rules

This feature facilitates automatic routing of an engagement based on specific conditions. For example, a tax return engagement may be routed automatically to the extra step of being put on extension if it is within a certain number of days before the due date. Another example would be to route complex returns to a pool of senior tax preparers for assignment.

Document and File Binder

The ability to access the electronic documents and files that are associated with the engagement is perhaps the most important feature of the workflow system. The optimal model for this is when you have a workflow system that integrates directly with a document management system. The key is to be able to directly access the files associated with the engagement as it moves through the office from within the workflow system. Think of the workflow system as the Redweld expanding file pocket with the routing sheet attached to it.

Review Note Tracking

This is a pretty important component of the whole paperless workflow model. When we take away the paper, we are also taking away the pencils. So you need to establish what your process will be for recording and tracking review notes. Some firms use Excel spreadsheets or Word documents. We are not big fans of either approach. We believe that you need to have a more structured process for managing review notes, and using workflow software is the logical way to do this. You should look for the ability to track notes by category or type and track the entire thread of a note until it is cleared. You also need to determine how you want to manage the purging of all or selected notes.

Electronic Forms, Checklists, and Routing Sheets

These features collectively give you the ability to complete the transition to paperless workflows by accommodating all the documents that you utilize to manage and track an engagement. You just need to make sure that, at a minimum, the workflow system can accommodate all the supplemental forms that you use to process your engagements.

E-mail Alerts

Most of us will agree that e-mail is both a curse and a blessing. But if we use the tools that are at our disposal to automate the management of e-mail messages, they can be a very effective way to communicate. When it comes to workflow systems, we need the e-mail alerts to notify us when an engagement has been routed to us or to notify clients when they have a new document posted to their portal or the status of their engagement has changed. The ability to setup various types of e-mail notifications is an important feature of an effective workflow system.

Management Reports

One of the key features of workflow software is the ability to generate a variety of management reports to monitor and manage all your firm's engagements and your staff assignments. The beautiful part of this is that the reports are available simply as a by-product of using the software to manage the engagement flow. Review figure 10-3, which shows a sample report from the FirmFlow system from Thomson-Reuters that integrates with the GoFileRoom document management system.

Figure 10-3: *Thomson-Reuter's GoFileRoom Firm Flow Workflow Software*

Source: Used with permission from the Tax & Accounting business of Thomson Reuters.

Based on our experience of helping numerous CPA firms to go paperless, we have found that the workflow application is one of the most useful and practical applications to implement. Everyone from the administrative staff to the managing partner will appreciate having access to client engagement information at the click of the mouse. You can use table 10-1 as a checklist to evaluate workflow software.

Table 10-1: *Workflow Software Selection Checklist*

✓ Simple and intuitive interface
✓ Integration with a document management system
✓ Set up multiple workflows
✓ Create customized checklists
✓ Create customized data fields for tracking information unique to your firm
✓ Schedule routing assignments in advance
✓ Maintain detailed routing history
✓ Establish access permission controls
✓ Record and manage review notes
✓ Configurable e-mail notifications
✓ Configurable engagement statuses
✓ Integration with practice management software
✓ Process engagement setup in bulk
✓ Maintain all information pertinent to tracking an engagement
✓ Integration with portal application
✓ Mobile device support
✓ Customizable engagement status and tracking reports

It is unlikely you will find a solution that provides all the preceding features, so make sure that the core components are there and evaluate the vendor's history of product enhancements. Workflow software is still in its infancy, so you should expect the scope of features and functions in the application to evolve in the coming years, particularly as it relates to integrating with mobile devices.

Chapter 11

Cloud-Based Client Accounting System

We have covered a lot of territory in this book to help guide you through the transformation to a 21st century digital practice model. We talked specifically about how your client portal can fundamentally change the way you service your clients by acting as their gateway to cloud computing. The concept of offering a shared, cloud-based accounting system to your clients opens up a whole new frontier of opportunities to improve and expand the services you offer them. This is a true win-win service for you and your clients.

The concept, shown in figure 11-1, is to offer your clients the opportunity to access their accounting system directly through your portal and provide shared access to their system by your firm so that you can provide the appropriate level of oversight and assistance to your clients in real time without having to transfer data files back and forth.

Figure 11-1: *The Cloud-Based Accounting System Paradigm*

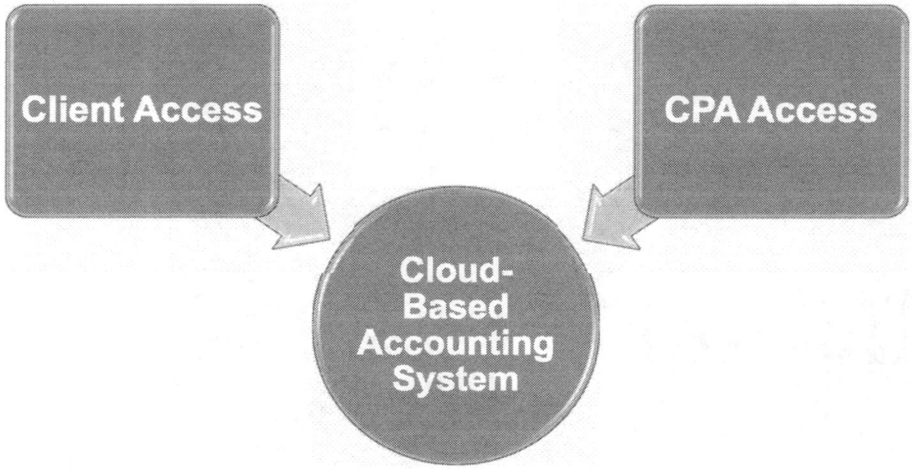

It Is Time for a Change

Think for a few moments about how much the information-sharing model has changed with the evolution of technology in recent years. We have talked extensively about the cloud and all the benefits it brings to information services. This is the opportunity for CPA practitioners to fully embrace and leverage the concept. Think about the traditional model that has evolved over the past 20 years with PC-based accounting and bookkeeping systems. This is depicted in figure 11-2.

Figure 11-2: *The Traditional PC-Based Accounting System Paradigm*

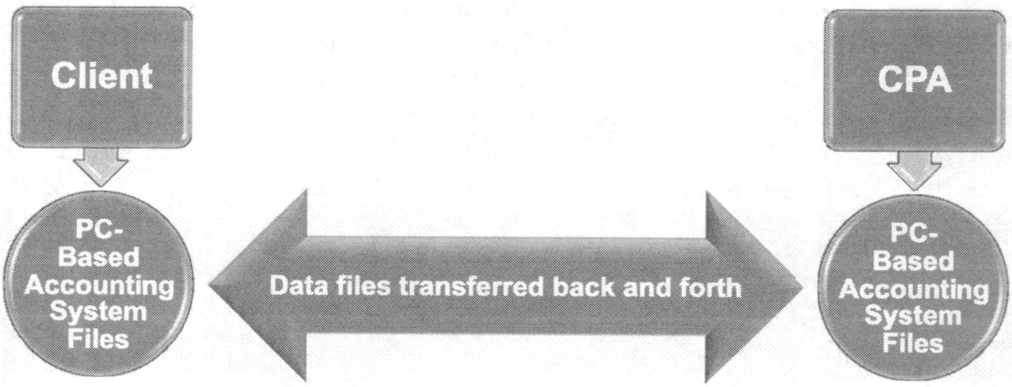

Inefficiencies With the Traditional Client Accounting Model

Some inefficiencies of the traditional client accounting model are as follows:

- Labor intensive transfer of data files between the client and CPA
- Privacy vulnerabilities resulting from file transfer via e-mail, USB drives, and so forth
- Accounting data out of sync between client copy and CPA copy
- Purchasing and managing multiple versions of the same software to support multiple clients
- Inability to access client system on demand to provide oversight and analysis of key performance indicators (KPIs)
- Accounting reports transferred via e-mail
- Weakness in internal controls

Much Improved Service With the Cloud Accounting Model

Some ways that the cloud accounting model can improve service for your clients are as follows:

- Real-time access to the client's accounting system on demand
- Eliminate labor-intensive transfer of accounting data files
- Minimize breach of privacy vulnerabilities via encrypted access
- Accounting data files stored in a data center with world class security and disaster recovery protection
- Always on current version of the software
- Increased responsibility and accountability of the software vendor for system reliability and performance
- Most importantly, the opportunity to provide clients with an array of options for helping them maximize the use of their accounting and financial information

When we advise firms on this concept, we often hear many reasons why they are not prepared to pursue this initiative. However, the more you come to understand all that this model has to offer, you will realize the opportunity it provides to offer your clients a better service. There is little question in our minds that this is the direction the market is moving. The question you have to ask yourself is whether you want to be an early adapter and demonstrate to your clients that your firm leverages emerging technologies to enhance your services to them.

The Opportunity

The potential opportunity is if your firm establishes an alliance of sorts with a Web-based accounting system vendor, you can pursue a number of alternative paths to enhance your client accounting services with this shared accounting system model. You may want to refer to the two-part panel discussion that was published in the February and March, 2012 issues of the *Journal of Accountancy* to learn how some innovative firms are successfully pursuing this model. Of course, it depends on your firm's overall strategy regarding how far you may want to go down this path. But we believe that it can lead to a higher quality of service to your clients, increased efficiency in your accounting services workflows, and increased profitability for your practice. Who would not want to pursue those objectives?

The following points paint a picture of how you might go about the process of implementing a strategy to offer a cloud-based accounting solution to your clients:

1. Research the market of cloud-based CPA/client shared accounting systems, for example, Intacct (www.intacct.com), and learn what this model is all about. Refer to appendix C, "Resource Center," for a list of potential solutions.
2. Evaluate your client accounting services to determine where there is an opportunity to enhance these services by providing the cloud-based accounting system platform to your clients.
3. You may want to offer a variety of services wrapped around this concept:
   a. **Simple compilation engagements.** Let the client fulfill his or her traditional bookkeeping role by doing all the transaction processing and bringing it to the point of an unadjusted trial balance at the end of the period (monthly, quarterly, or annually). Your accounting personnel will then login to the system directly, analyze the trial balance, make the necessary reclassification and adjust journal entries to bring it to a completed trial balance that feeds into an accurate set of financial statement reports. Shuffling data files would be eliminated, and the service would be expedited.
   b. **Outsourced accounting services.** With this model, you would meet with your client to review his or her core accounting processes and determine which processes, or pieces of a process, they want to outsource to you, for example, processing payroll checks and payroll tax reports or classifying and processing vendor invoices and payments. One of the key advantages of a cloud-based system is that it is relatively easy to facilitate shared transaction and reporting processes. This provides you with an unprecedented opportunity to demonstrate your commitment to helping your clients with their accounting tasks according to their needs and objectives.
   c. **Virtual CFO service.** A niche service that can be provided with this model is to offer your clients a service whereby you monitor their financial KPIs by accessing their system remotely and analyzing the data. You can provide them with a monthly analysis from your perspective and some actions they may want to consider taking based on your analysis. You can also set up some real time financial

dashboards that will make it easier for your clients to monitor their KPIs themselves. Remember the pyramid back in chapter 1, "The Nature of the Digital Practice Model and the Benefits to You and Your Firm"? This is a prime example of automating the red zone services and replacing them with more valuable green zone advisory services that leverage your expertise.

The Economic Model

This is a good place to discuss the need to address your fee model as you increase the automation of your services and extend the reach of them directly to your client. We suspect you have heard plenty over the years about moving from hourly-based billing to value-priced fee models. This is the time to give more serious consideration to this model because your clients will perceive the value of this type of service based on the benefits to them. They do not particularly care how many hours of effort it takes on your part, unlike when you are billing them by the hour. Instead, they will evaluate the service offering you are proposing and the fee you have established and decide whether it is worth it to them. If you structure your service offering properly, it should be a very straightforward decision on their part.

We can only speak from experience on this concept. When we established our firm in 2001, one of our core tenets was to never bill by the hour. Instead, we always develop proposals that outline the services we are proposing to offer and what the fee is. In the 10 plus years of our existence, we have never billed by the hour. Clients and prospective clients have always demonstrated an appreciation for this model. They do not want to have to monitor our internal efficiencies in providing their services. Instead, they monitor whether we are delivering the value that they anticipated when they signed up for the service. This gives us every incentive to be as efficient as possible and to stay focused on the quality of the service we are delivering. We do not win every engagement proposal, but that probably means we are in the right fee range for our services. There is a significant by-product benefit of this model; our cash flow is much more stable, the billing process is greatly simplified, and collection issues are minimized. This is such an important time to consider making this transformation because the opportunity to reduce your labor efforts via automation through the cloud is unprecedented, and you will find that the services you are providing are at a higher value level. As one small example, just think how much time your staff is currently spending just to transfer the accounting system data files back and forth.

We encourage you to visit the cloud accounting vendors listed in appendix C and participate in a Web-based demonstration of their offerings and begin to develop a knowledge base of this concept.

Chapter 12

Security and Disaster Recovery

Dealing with IT security and disaster recovery is analogous to going to the dentist's office. We do not typically want to deal with the whole experience, but we know it is a necessary part of good personal healthcare and hygiene. This chapter is not meant to be a technical discussion about information security and disaster recovery protection, but rather a description of a series of practical best practices you can implement to secure the privacy and integrity of the data your firm retains. We cover IT security and disaster recovery together because many of the pieces you need to implement overlap both initiatives because they protect against intentional and accidental data loss or destruction. It is important to understand the components required to implement a comprehensive data protection model, such as hardware devices, software applications, policies and procedures, and personnel training. The latter two are arguably the pieces that have the greatest impact on whether you achieve success or failure in this endeavor.

In order to develop an effective IT security model in your firm, you have to assess the risk of exposure to each of the vulnerabilities listed in figure 12-1. This is much easier said than done. The key is to implement best practice, mainstream protections that will push you above the negligence stage. This will put your firm in a position that will demonstrate to your clients and other interested parties that you are taking prudent steps to protect their confidential information. Perhaps more importantly, your firm will also be in compliance

Figure 12-1: *IT Security Vulnerabilities*

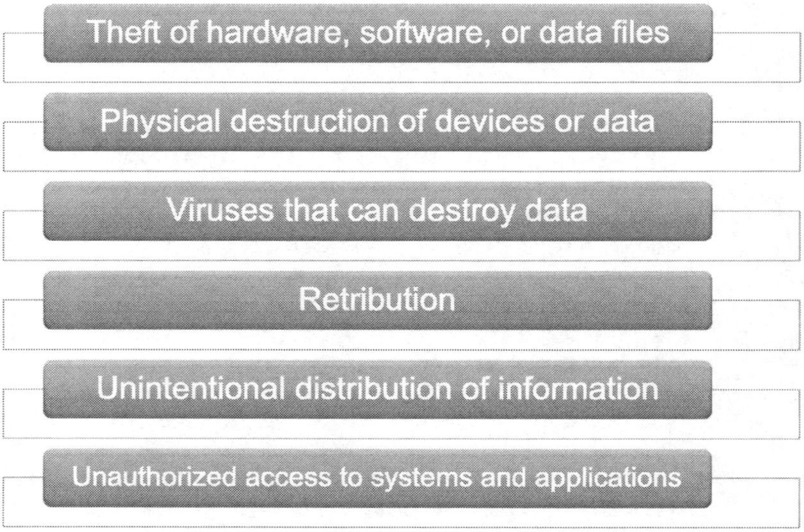

with the vast array of privacy regulations that cover your practice. In our efforts to make this initiative as painless as possible, we have outlined a multistep approach (illustrated in figure 12-2) to developing and implementing an effective security model for your firm.

Data Security Strategies

Figure 12-2: *Data Security Strategies*

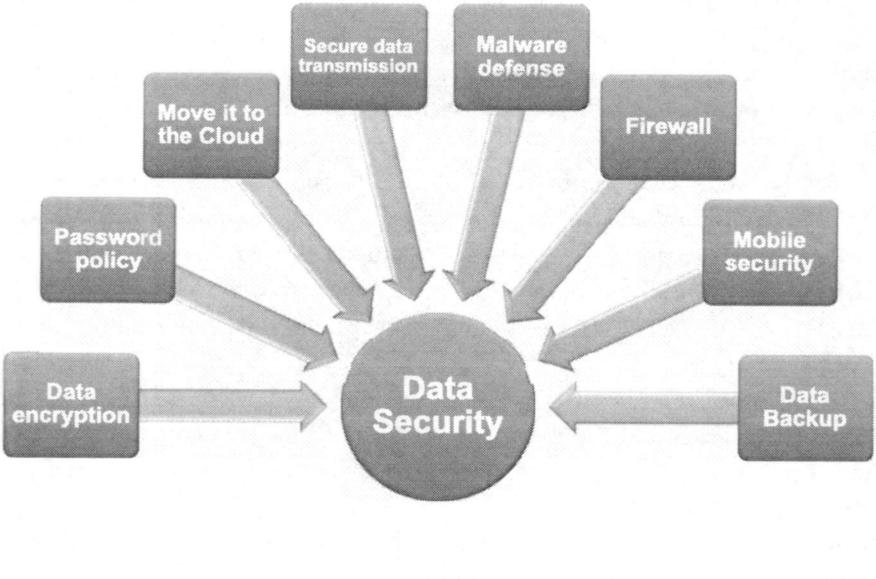

Data Encryption

If you read the specifications for virtually any data privacy legislation or regulation, you will find a requirement that personal data be encrypted at all times. Regardless of the regulatory environment, it is simply a good business practice to follow. A simple definition of *encryption* is the process of converting standard plain text data files, that is, e-mail messages, PDF files, and Excel spreadsheets, into encoded files that cannot be deciphered without a decoding key, typically a password. Versions of an unencrypted Excel file are shown in figure 12-3.

Figure 12-3: *Unencrypted Excel File (left) and Encrypted Excel File (right)*

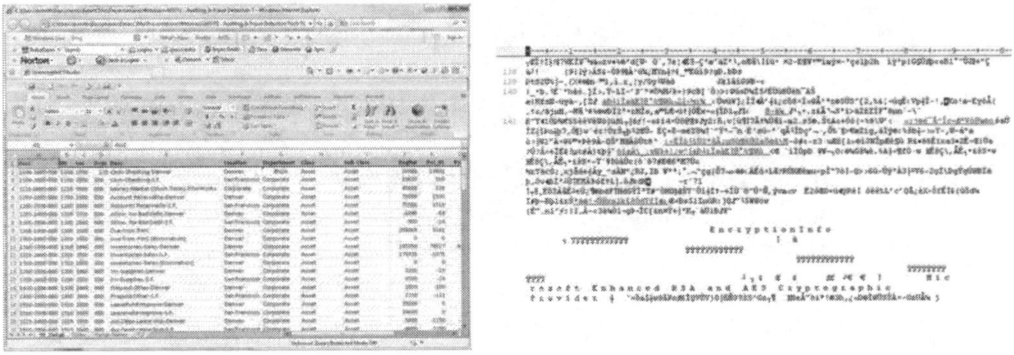

Source: Microsoft Excel. Used with permission from Microsoft.

Ideally, your sensitive data should be encrypted at all times, but especially when it is stored on stationary or portable devices and when it is in transmission. More specifically, your data should be encrypted at the following points:

- On network server drives
- On desktop/laptop drives
- On USB and other portable drives
- On tablets and smartphones
- In E-mail file attachments

Abundant solutions are available for encrypting all your storage devices with a single software solution. The new generation of Windows Server and Windows 7 operating systems offer an encryption feature called BitLocker that will work across all your storage devices. We strongly recommend that you seek the guidance of a professional with experience in this area to help you implement your encryption model. Refer to appendix C, "Resource Center," for links to additional encryption solutions.

> "Some of the largest and medium-sized U.S. airports report close to 637,000 laptops lost each year, according to the Ponemon Institute Survey."
>
> PC World June 2008

Some very basic steps can be taken for encrypting e-mail. You can encrypt any MS Office 2007 and 2010 file within those applications by applying a password. The same opportunity exists with Adobe Acrobat and PDF files. As long as the body of the e-mail message does not contain confidential data, this is a practical method for encryption. Just be sure that you do not communicate the password in an unprotected e-mail (see the section "Password Policy" that follows). If you want to use a more complete e-mail encryption model that protects both the message and the attached files, you can utilize a program such as PGP Desktop E-mail from Symantec (www.symantec.com/PGP).

Password Policy

Perhaps the best known and most talked about security policy is that of passwords. Most systems require a password as a form of authentication to access a system or application. The SANS Institute, a nationally recognized computer security training and certification organization, provides a best practice password policy. Their recommendations include the following:

- Change passwords on a quarterly basis
- Contain at least three of the following characters: lowercase letters, uppercase letters, numbers, punctuation, and special symbols
- Minimum of 15 characters
- No words found in the dictionary
- Never written down or shared with another individual
- Use different passwords for various systems, accounts, and applications

In order to create the strongest password, it should be completely random. In recent years, there have been discussions of using pass phrases instead of passwords. The advantages are that they can be longer and easier to remember. A pass phrase is something like: "This is the first day of the rest of your life." It usually contains words separated by spaces, but it can also contain symbols or misspelled words, such as "Thi$ 1s the fir$t dae of the re$t of ur lief."

A pass phrase can be even better with totally random words with special characters such as "@pple B@ll Or@nge Bike Lime Run." The idea is to create passwords that meet system requirements but are easy to remember. You can even create a systematic means to use the same pass phrase for all websites or applications by adding something related to each particular website or application to the end of your pass phrase (or password for that matter.) If you use pass phrases, you should pick something easy to remember but not a common phrase or saying. You may find you are limited by the password parameters of the source application.

All these guidelines sound great in theory but are very difficult in practice to implement. If you create a 15-character password that uses a unique and random combination of characters, how are you going to remember it without writing it down, especially if it is different for each application? That is where password memorization programs come to the rescue. One such application is RoboForm (www.roboform.com). RoboForm will store login information for all your websites and applications in a single encrypted file. All you need to do is remember one complex master password to open the encrypted password file. The key to using any of these programs is to make sure your master password that encrypts the data file is very strong. These programs facilitate creating highly complex passwords that you can change often because you do not have to remember them. The newest version of RoboForm also integrates with your biometrics (fingerprint reader) if you have one installed, whereby your master password can be entered via your fingerprint match. These programs typically sell for around $30 per user, which is a relatively small price to pay for peace of mind.

Cloud Computing

We covered cloud computing extensively in chapter 3, 'Infrastructure." The point we want to emphasize here is that cloud applications typically provide the most sophisticated physical and technical security protections that money can buy. They are managed by highly skilled IT security professionals. In addition, cloud applications provide the ability to have your data available anytime, anywhere, thus, eliminating the need to keep data floating around on your portable devices. Just connect to the cloud when you need to access it. This also means that your data resides in a single location; therefore you only need to worry about securing data in that location.

The following is a list of the typical security and disaster recovery safeguards that are provided by data center service providers that host all the various forms of cloud computing infrastructure services outlined in chapter 3.

- Electrical power system that is fully redundant containing uninterrupted power systems (UPS) with back-up generators that include 24 hours of on-site fuel.
- Dedicated and redundant HVAC systems.
- Waterless fire suppression system.
- Multilevel physical security protection.
  - Cement or brick building with no windows.
  - No signage describing that a data center is on-site.
  - Closed-circuit TV system that monitors all access points and data center with recording system.

- — Cameras directed by motion sensors to follow and track movement within the data center.
- — Biometric, key card, and code access required to enter datacenter at all times.
- — Alarm system with fail-safe mechanisms to prevent false discharge or tampering of the system.
- — Database of individuals authorized to access the facility.
- — Database of individuals accessing the facility.
- — All racks of servers and equipment are locked with entry via key card and access code.

- Network operations center that is used to view and monitor the entire data center, including physical security, environmental systems, and all data center equipment 24 hours a day,7 days a week, 365 days a year.
- Multiple and redundant access to telecommunications providers.
- Networks are secured with firewalls, intrusion detection system, and intrusion prevention systems.
- Redundant and real time data center that provides automatic fail-over in case the main data center goes down.
- Trained staff of technical specialists.

When evaluating a data center, you should ask for independent validation of the security controls. The data center should be able to provide various "audit" tests or reports. These include penetration tests, security audits, and the AICPA's Service Organization Controls (SOC) reports (formerly known as SAS No. 70 reports). The new SOC reports (SOC 1, SOC 2, and SOC 3) not only report on controls at a service organization (data center) that are likely to be relevant to an audit of a user entity's financial statement (what SAS No. 70 was designed to do) but also report on the effectiveness of these controls related to operations and compliance. So when evaluating a data center, look for a SOC 2 report, which specifically addresses one or more of the 5 key system attributes: security, availability, processing integrity, confidentiality, and privacy.

Secure Data Transmission

We addressed the issue of encrypting files when they are stored and transmitted via e-mail, but what about data that we enter on a website, for example, accounting transactions, payroll data, personal information, and so forth? For this, you need to verify that you are connecting through a secure transmission, which means your data is encrypted as it travels across the Internet to and from its destination. The most popular method is called secure socket layer or SSL. This process encrypts all data that is exchanged between your browser and the Web server you are communicating with. You can confirm SSL is active if the URL of the Web server you are communicating with begins with https://, the "s" represents secure. You should never enter any personal information through your browser, including credit card information, unless you see the https://prefix.

Antivirus Software

Antivirus software will help protect your computer from malware (an abbreviation for malicious software), which is the greatest threat to most information systems. *Malware* are programs that are designed to gain unauthorized access to your computer and applications or to destroy your data one way or another. The most common forms of malware include the following:

- **Viruses.** Malicious programs that find their way into your computer via e-mail messages, attached to files, or through website access. A virus can wreak havoc on your computer and will often spread to other devices attached to your network or are forwarded on to others.
- **Worms.** A unique type of virus that essentially replicates itself continuously to the point that it slows down the performance of your computer in every aspect.
- **Trojan horses.** This is a malicious program that appears disguised as a legitimate program, for example, a calculator utility. It is a form of virus that will corrupt your data files.
- **Spyware.** As the name implies, this is a program that finds its way onto your computer and will then capture information such as login keystrokes, credit card data, websites visited, and so forth. The spyware can then transmit this information to a remote computer.

The good news is that in the face of all these threats, there are some very reliable antivirus programs that can provide complete protection from all the threats listed previously. Some of the more well-known providers are Norton, McAfee, and Kaspersky. In order to prevent malware infection, all computers should have antivirus software installed.

There are basically three components of anti-virus software:

1. The software application, which is installed on the computer.
2. The virus definitions, which is a database downloaded from the antivirus software developer, installed on the computer, and updated on a frequent basis as new threats are identified.
3. The service, which is a program that stays active on the computer whenever it is running. This is your front line of protection.

It is important that the service is never removed, disabled, or stopped. During installation of some applications, it will be recommended that you disable the antivirus software. This should never be done because it could provide a moment when malware can attack the unprotected system. The virus definitions database should also be kept up-to-date. Most antivirus software vendors provide at least weekly virus definition updates. We recommend that you perform regular audits of workstations to confirm that all workstations have antivirus software installed, the definitions are current, and the service is running. You must inform your staff that this software is never to be halted or disabled.

Firewalls

There are many technical terms for *firewalls*, but simply speaking, they are hardware devices that reside between your internal network and the Internet. Their job is to make sure only permitted traffic from the Internet passes through to your internal network. Firewalls utilize complex rules, which means you tell the firewall what to allow and what to deny in terms of the type of data traffic. Traffic includes things like Web browsing, e-mail, chatting, remote desktop access, and file transfer, to name a few. The firewall basically looks at the traffic to determine if it meets an allowable rule and, if so, passes it along to the network. A good IT audit exercise is to ask your IT service provider to print a list of all the rules and explain what each ones does. It will be immediately apparent that firewall management requires a unique base of knowledge. For that reason, you typically need to seek the services of a system engineer who specializes in this area.

As with all the services we have discussed in this book, there are software as a service (SaaS) solutions for firewall management. This is typically a core service that is available from a managed service provider, as we discussed in chapter 3. There are also personal firewalls, which are typically integrated into the antimalware applications we discussed previously. These are quasi-managed services because the rules are updated by the vendor as part of the virus threat databases. The bottom line on firewalls is that they are a key component of your IT security and require special technical expertise, so be sure to consult with outside IT professionals.

Mobile Computing Security

This is becoming an increasingly complex issue to deal with as the deployment of smartphones and tablets grows exponentially. These devices often have full access to the company database. The first step is to determine if the specific devices have built-in encryption or if it is available as an app. You can, and should, install antivirus software on these devices. In addition, you can secure your smartphones or tablets with a lock code to prevent unauthorized access. These are similar to a PIN, but there are various options to make them even more secure. Most of these portable devices can be easily connected to a USB port on any computer. This allows the user to copy any information from your system to his or her device. We recommend that you create a policy that states only authorized company devices can be connected to company computers. In cases when security is of utmost importance, we recommend that you disable all USB ports on computers to prevent unauthorized file transfers.

Remote wipe is another safeguard for your portable devices. This is an application that allows you to issue a command that will remotely wipe all the information from a lost or stolen device. The key weakness of this feature is that the lost device needs to be connected to the data network before it will actually get wiped. Device tracking is yet another tool that will track the location of your device. Many smartphones have this built in, but you can also buy a service called LoJack that will provide device tracking for laptops.

Data Backup

This has been a standard operating procedure since computer technology was first introduced. The good news is that today there is an abundance of alternative data back-up solutions that are very reliable and relatively inexpensive. Three main things need to be backed up: data files, software application files, and configuration settings files. The data files are obviously the most critical; they need to be backed up to a redundant storage device, at a minimum, on a daily basis. With all the cloud-based storage services available, it is very practical to set up a back-up process that is done continuously via the Internet with encrypted transmission. These services can typically be programmed to work in the background to minimize the strain on your system during normal operations.

Our recommendation is that you rely on a cloud-based storage service for all your system storage devices, including server, PC, smartphone, and tablet drives. The benefit is that you will have peace of mind knowing that all your data is located in a secure data center with world class protections in place. As one simple example, we use the Carbonite SaaS service to back up all our computers. They offer a pricing model of $599 for 500 GB of cumulative data storage for up to 15 devices. It does background backups, so no file is typically more than a couple of hours old before it is backed up. One of the key benefits of the online storage model is that if we lose a computer, we can go out and buy a new one, login to Carbonite, and download the files from the lost computer. Refer to appendix C for links to a number of online back-up storage services. They are not all the same, so do your due diligence. Because we are 100 percent cloud-based at our firm, all our applications data is stored at the SaaS vendors' data centers, so we have 100 percent protection with virtually no effort.

Whatever back-up system you use, it is imperative that you do a fire drill test on a periodic basis, at least every 90 days. Simply try to restore a file or group of files from the back-up storage and observe the process to make sure it works effectively and according to your expectations. The most important thing to verify is that all the files are getting backed up. You do not want to discover a deficiency after you have experienced a loss of data.

Disaster Recovery Protection

We could write a lengthy discussion about disaster recovery protection. Theoretically, every organization should have a disaster recovery plan (DRP). In reality, only a small percentage of organizations have a DRP that is documented and tested on a regular basis. In a perfect world, every organization would make this a priority. For most of us, however, we have too many other priorities to juggle, so you have to make sure you have covered the basics. We have outlined a simplistic approach you can take to ensure you have a solid disaster recovery plan:

1. Utilize a data center hosting service for all your server infrastructure and data storage. Be sure that the service provider backs up the data to a redundant data center on a real time basis.
2. Utilize SaaS cloud applications as much as practical to get disaster recovery protection as a by-product of the service.
3. Implement online storage for all your personal computers and mobile devices.
4. Develop an action plan for replacing all lost, stolen, or damaged equipment. This should include an inventory of the make, model, and serial number of all devices; a data file storage catalog so you know what files are stored where; and procedures for doing a system restore.

Chapter 13

Developing and Implementing Your Technology Plan

What Do I Do Now?

At this point, we have discussed all the things you can, and should, do to put your firm on a solid footing for the new digital age. It would be easy to say that there is just too much to do, throw in the towel, and just address your IT needs on an ad hoc basis as situations present themselves. Believe it or not, that is actually the most time-consuming and expensive approach and yields the poorest results. It may not seem that way because there is no real measurement of success or accountability. Alternatively, taking a strategic approach and investing the time to develop your plan will provide significant results in terms of optimizing your allocation of time and financial resources and getting the highest return on investment in terms of workflow efficiency, quality of client service, and profitability.

The CPA/client paradigm is entering a period of significant transformation as a result of the shifting IT paradigm to cloud-based and mobile computing. The reason we covered so much material in this book is because it is all interrelated. The closer you get to putting all the pieces of the puzzle together, the more you will begin to see the value of the whole picture. The key is to approach your IT strategy and deployment in a methodical manner, which we will describe in this chapter.

> **"In preparing for battle I have always found that plans are useless, but planning is indispensable."**
>
> **General Dwight D. Eisenhower**

How Do I Approach the Process?

Whether you are a general in the army or a bricklayer, there is no disputing the fact that developing a plan is key to success. Here we will provide you with a process for developing and executing your plan. At a macro level, five key steps need to be addressed to complete the IT planning cycle. These steps are illustrated in figure 13-1.

Figure 13-1: *IT Planning Cycle*

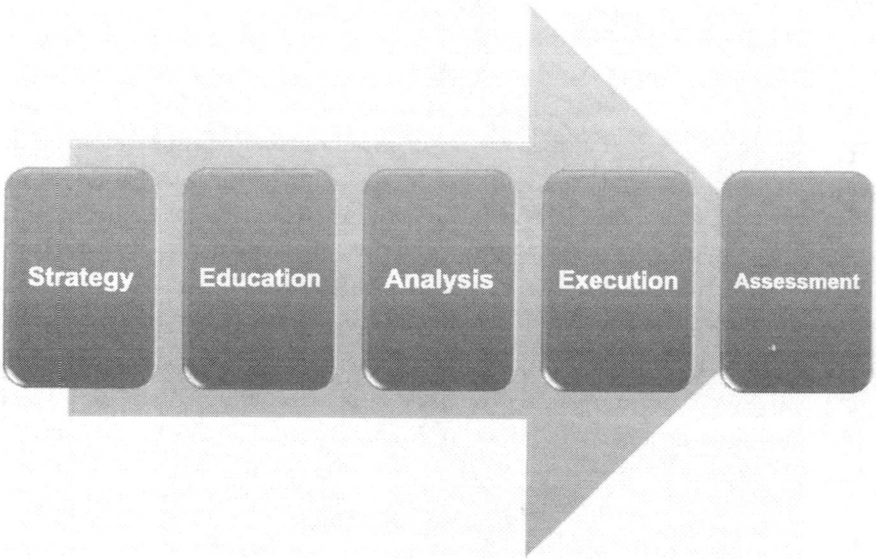

Strategy

The first step in developing the optimal IT plan for your practice is deciding in what direction you want your practice to go. You and your partners may already have this figured out, or you have an idea in your head about the future of your firm, or you may have been too busy working in the business at the expense of working on the business. Take some time to formulate your strategy. It is your most important responsibility as a leader of your firm. This does not have to be a long, drawn out, and expensive process. If it is done properly, it can be accomplished over a few meetings that should not last more than two or three hours each. If you spend more time than that in strategy meetings, you will incur the law of diminishing returns. Having more meetings of shorter duration will yield much better results than sitting in a room for a couple of days trying to figure it all out. You cannot underestimate the value of the time required to think things through between planning sessions to get clarity on your thoughts and decisions.

- Strategy is about **where** you are going.
- Planning is about **how** you are going to get there.
- A plan without a strategy is an oxymoron.

Five key things you should try to resolve in establishing your firm strategy without regard to technology are as follows:

- Target client demographics, such as industries, location, size, stage, and so forth.
- Service offerings, such as tax, accounting, write-up, financial planning, and so forth
- Staffing skills, experience, location, and roles
- Marketing, including messaging, branding, and methodology
- Economics, including revenue metrics, fee model, compensation model, and capital investments

Keep in mind that these items are addressed at a macro level. Do not get caught in the trap of trying to figure out all the details at this stage. Your strategic planning process will crash and burn. Ideally, you can come out of this process with a very simple picture of your strategy. Many expert strategic planners will advise you that your strategic plan should be limited to a one-page document that everyone in the organization can easily understand.

A very simple example would be a strategic plan that looks something like this:

- **Mission.** Our firm will be the premier provider of small business and personal tax return services throughout our state. We will provide no attest services and will stick close to our core competencies.
- **Target client demographics.** Partnerships, limited liability companies, and individuals with a focus on professional service businesses throughout the state of [*name of state*].
- **Service offerings.** Tax planning and compliance at the federal, state, and local level. Client accounting services will be offered, ranging from a complete virtual accounting service to process all accounting transactions and appropriate financial reporting, to basic year-end trial balance and financial statement processing. We will refer out all services outside of our core competencies, such as international tax compliance and attestation services.
- **Staffing.** Technical competency and interpersonal skills will be our primary qualifiers for hiring at all position levels. Administrative staff must have a proven track record of attention to detail, responsibility, and positive working relationships. Entry level professional staff must have an undergraduate accounting degree with a cumulative GPA of 3.4 or higher, with some degree of work experience during college years, and must be committed to becoming a CPA. Non-entry level professional staff must be CPAs with verifiable references that will attest to their technical competency and interpersonal communication skills.
- **Marketing.** Our message to the market will be that we are a firm that provides the highest level of professionalism and quality in the services that we provide and that our primary goal is to help our clients achieve success. Our reputation will be established as a high quality firm, not a low fee provider. We will use all methods of marketing communications, that is, personal and business event networking, community support, e-mail, and social media.
- **Economics.** Our core economic premise is that we have to establish a fee model that will support our ability to provide top quality service, which requires us to provide a competitive compensation program that will allow us to hire the best and the brightest. We are committed to a value pricing fee model. This means that for all engagements, we will develop a clear and concise statement of work and establish a fair value fee for the engagement that provides the requisite level of compensation for the quality of our staff, quality control of the engagement, and a fair return on our investment in the firm. We will leverage our portal to provide pass-through information and services that will provide value to our clients and revenue to the firm.

The preceding text is a very simple example of a one-page strategic plan that covers the essence of what we want the firm to be about. Even in this simplistic form, it can provide invaluable guidance in prioritizing and executing your IT initiatives. Just the mere fact of asking how any given IT initiative will help to achieve any part of the strategic plan will help to establish a value for the initiative. This strategy phase should be limited to the current and emerging firm leaders because they are the primary stakeholders and decision makers.

Retaining the services of an outside facilitator to keep this process focused on the objective is usually a worthwhile investment.

Education

The education phase of the IT planning cycle is all about learning what your options are for leveraging technology in your practice. This is an ongoing process but is something you should focus on as you get ready to develop your technology plan. Our hope is that this book and the accompanying "Resource Center" in appendix C will go a long way toward raising your awareness of all the tools and services that are available to automate your practice and enhance your client services. Other ways to educate yourself on these topics include attending CPA technology continuing education programs (seminars, conferences, and webinars) and researching CPA technology vendor websites and watching some of the demos they have posted. We are constantly amazed at how much quality information is available without even having to leave your desk. Do not forget about the various accounting and tax technology publications, such as the *CPA Practice Advisor* (www.cpapracticeadvisor.com).

In our opinion, the very best way to get educated is to visit with other practitioners. Find out what is working for them and what has caused them problems. Realize that every organization has had at least some bad experiences with technology, so be sure to get a second or third opinion if you are evaluating a particular hardware, software, or service provider. We also recommend that you assign multiple people with the task of getting themselves educated on specified topics, so that they can report back to the group what they have learned. Having a diversity of input in the planning process is invaluable.

Analysis

The first two steps are all about determining where you want to go as a firm and what your range of available technology solutions are. This is the step when you start to roll up the shirt sleeves and begin the process of developing your technology plan. The objective of this step is to conduct a SWOT (strengths, weaknesses, opportunities, and threats) assessment of sorts that assesses your current business model from a workflow efficiency perspective and your overall IT model. This includes hardware, software applications, and both internal and external service providers.

As far as a methodology for this process, it's time to talk about the team. This process should never be a one man, or woman, endeavor. Even if you are a sole practitioner, at a minimum, you should get involvement from your IT services provider. Ideally, your team will include representatives from each of your core service lines, firm administration, IT services, and a member of the firm ownership with authority to represent all the partners and shareholders. The latter is important because you want the team to have a frame of reference about what the limits are during the planning process. Nothing is more disillusioning than going through the process of analysis and developing recommendations only to be rejected without good cause. The shareholder liaison can buffer the expectations during the planning process. One of the team members needs to be designated as the champion of the process to facilitate scheduling and keep the process on a timeline. Generally, the firm administrator is the optimal person to champion the process because he or she will typically have a broad perspective on the firm's operations from every angle.

Once the team is assembled, the analysis process should begin with the facilitation of a "brain dump" session by the team about what is working well, what is not, where the primary workflow bottlenecks are, and what the labor-intensive tasks are. This information then needs to be analyzed and prioritized about what issues are most important to address or will provide the greatest opportunity for improved workflow efficiency. Many types of tools are available for this process. At our firm, CPA Crossings, we use a methodology called McNellis Compression Planning® (www.mcnellisco.com). This system provides a structured process for conducting virtually any type of planning session in a compressed time frame of typically two to three hours per session. We have included an example of an actual IT assessment that we conducted for a small firm in Appendix A. You will see how practical and informative the results are.

The next part of this phase is to conduct a second planning session to analyze the results from the previous session with the priorities that were identified and match them up with each of the 10 steps to a digital practice outlined in this book. You should see a pattern form very quickly that will identify the easiest things that can be done to achieve the maximum level of improvement. You should organize your initiatives into four categories: infrastructure, CPA toolkit, software applications, and workflow.

The deliverable from this process should be a relatively straight-forward plan that identifies what initiatives are to be undertaken over the next 6–12 months, 12–24 months, and beyond. There is not much point in developing a detailed plan beyond the next 24 months. Things will change along the way, such as changes to your business environment, the introduction of new technologies, personnel turnover, and so forth. Keep the focus on the short term and what defines success. Getting small steps accomplished can have a big impact on the overall success of your plan implementation. Taking on too much can be overwhelming and result in failed initiatives and disillusionment.

There is no silver bullet here. Every firm is in a very different place in terms of what is working and what is not at any given point in time. So the key here is to focus on the process, and the results should become relatively clear. If you struggle to come out of this process with a clear roadmap of priorities, it would be a prudent investment to retain an outside facilitator, as was recommended for the strategic planning phase.

Execution

This is all about getting things done at a micro level, in the order of priority established. The effort required here is in direct relation to the scope of the initiative. Implementing dual monitors is an initiative that can easily be completed in a matter of days, whereas fully integrating a document management system can take months, if not years, to complete. Large or small, the execution of every initiative should follow a consistent pattern that includes the following steps:

- Definition of the initiative that includes what the overall objective is, what specific goals will be used to measure success, and what the deliverables and outcomes of the initiative will be.

- Identify a specific champion for the initiative. If it is an infrastructure initiative, then IT should champion it. On the other hand, if it is a software application or workflow redesign initiative, the champion should be someone more intimately familiar with the specific business processes affected by the initiative.
- Develop a project plan for completing the initiative that includes a timeline, resource requirements, and task assignments. Going through the exercise of developing the project plan can be a real eye opener. You may find that what you thought to be a relatively simple project ends up being a 16–24 month initiative. This is the time to determine what is required so that everyone proceeds with their eyes wide open. What you need to be careful about in developing the plan is to avoid being too aggressive in your expectations of what it takes. Most initiatives take twice as long and are twice as expensive as was originally anticipated. This is when so many IT initiatives fail as a result of unrealistic expectations.
- A review of the business processes affected by the initiative should be mandatory. This is where you truly come to understand the impact of the initiative and identify all the important issues that need to be addressed before you go too far down the path. The key to this step is to understand where the bottlenecks and inefficiencies are in the process and how the new technology, hardware, or software is going to effect a positive change.
- Do your research and make sure you know what your options are and what you are getting into. Talk with as many vendors and practitioners as practical. The more you do, the more you will become educated about what works and what does not. This is much cheaper and more efficient than deploying a solution that is not a good fit.

Assessment

It might be fair to say that no initiative is ever complete, particularly if it is the deployment of a new software application or a fundamental redesign of a process. Often, you get to the end of an initiative and you are just happy that you arrived. However, chances are that not everything went as expected, or you didn't achieve all your expectations. You should make a point of revisiting an initiative approximately six months after it is first completed. This is a good time to go back and review your original objective(s) and success metrics to see if you are getting what you expected out of your investment. You should also revisit the affected business processes to assess whether you are reaping the full benefits of the initiative that you invested in, as well as to identify any opportunity to further improve the process with new or existing technology.

The bottom line is that you should spend at least a half day each year on each of your core processes to identify opportunities to improve and further automate them. This is a relatively small investment in continuous process improvement and will help to ensure that you continue to increase the quality, value, and profitability of your client services.

Chapter 14

Case Studies

Clark Nuber P.S.: Leveraging Confirmation Software to Streamline the Audit Process

Firm Profile: Clark Nuber P.S., Bellevue, Washington

Contact: Peter Henley, Chief Information Officer

Offices: 1

Partners: 17

Staff Size: 160 (70 audit/60 tax/30 administrative)

Services: Traditional audit and tax services, very strong not-for-profit practice.

Software Platform(s): CCH ProFx Engagement for audits, GoSystem RS Tax (hosted), CCH Practice Management, SharePoint for document management and workflow processing. The focus of this case study is on the firm's use of the Confirmation.com cloud-based software to automate the confirmation of cash, accounts payable, and accounts receivable balances in the audit process.

Background: Clark Nuber has taken an innovative approach to the audit confirmation process. As opposed to the traditional model of charging the audit team with responsibility for performing their own audit confirmations, the firm has implemented a centralized confirmation process. One individual, with a backup, is responsible for all confirmations and uses the Confirmation.com software. This is a classic example of the importance of "process" to leverage the power of the software tools. The auditors choose the accounts to confirm, and then administrative staff handles the process from there.

Confirmation.com is a Web-hosted system for processing payables, receivables, and bank confirmations electronically. The system facilitates sending electronic confirmation requests directly to banks and other participating entities to process the confirmation requests automatically and securely. Confirmation.com guarantees responses with an average turnaround time of two days.

Benefits Achieved

- Turnaround time on confirmations is much faster, minimizing confirmations as a potential bottleneck in the audit engagement.
- Reduction in the cost of the audit by transferring the confirmation responsibility from the audit professionals to the administrative staff.
- Savings achieved by eliminating postage and paper supplies.
- Improvement in administrative staff morale by putting them in a fee-generating role.
- Improvement in auditor morale by relieving them of a primarily administrative task.
- Minimized confirmations being routed to multiple personnel in the firm.
- Processing second requests on confirmations is normally a time-consuming process, but with Confirmation.com, it takes a matter of seconds to send out the second confirmation request.

Lessons Learned

- "Nothing went wrong."
- Centralize the confirmation process and get it away from the professionals.
- Don't get caught up doing a big fancy return on investment analysis because your costs go down the day you buy Confirmation.com. "If you are aware of the product, you should do it this month, not next year. It is easy to do and saves money right away."
- Everyone who saw it believed in it.
- Cost of the audit was reduced.
- Confirmation.com doesn't work with a lot of small banks.
- Clark Nuber does a lot of brokerage account confirmations. Confirmation.com is working to accommodate this market.
- If you have 500 confirmations and 450 are in Confirmation.com, do the rest manually.
- The smaller the firm, the bigger the benefit of Confirmation.com. It is a "killer app."

Juravel & Company, LLC: Client Portals

Firm Profile: Juravel & Company, LLC, Alpharetta, Georgia

Managing Partner: Philip M. Juravel, CPA

Firm Administrator: N/A

Offices: 1

Partners: 1

Staff Size: 2.5–3

Services: Primarily tax planning and preparation for entities and individuals

Software Platform(s): CCH ProFx product suite: Tax, Portal (software as a service platform [SaaS]), Intelliforms (SaaS), Intelliconnect (SaaS), Practice Management, Engagement, Scan (SaaS) with Autoflow.

Background: This is a typical, small firm focused on providing tax planning and preparation services. In addition to the proprietor, Philip Juravel, there is a full-time staff accountant, a part-time bookkeeper, a full-time administrative assistant, and a part-time scan operator during tax season.

Due to the primary focus on tax services, we thought the best way to present this case study is to provide an overview of the tax return preparation business process and the benefits of integrating the client portal into the process:

- Business returns—Gather data in either printout or electronic format, often QuickBooks files. A working paper binder is set up in ProFx Engagement. For most returns, it is a matter of rolling over the prior year engagement. When possible, the client trial balance data is imported directly. In the case of QuickBooks, the client's trial balance data is usually keyed in manually.
- All supporting documentation is stored in Engagement. If it arrives in paper form, it is scanned. Excel spreadsheets are kept in their native format so they can be rolled over and updated for the current year activity.
- When the trial balance is completed, Dynalink is used to automatically create an export file to transfer data directly into ProFx Tax. This is used for 100 percent of the engagements. A key benefit is that whenever a trial balance needs to be updated, the change automatically flows into the tax return once the link is established.
- Scanning for entity returns is primarily done on the front end. Paper documents may be used to record notes.
- When the return is completed, it is submitted via e-file, and a client copy and the invoice are published directly to the portal. The accountant's copy stays in Engagement, and the client's copy goes to the portal.
- Individual returns—Some individuals upload a PDF copy of all documents to the portal. In that case, the firm downloads them to the local desktop and combines them

into a single PDF file. The PDF is converted to a TIFF (tagged image file format) for upload to ProFx Scan (SaaS) with Autoflow technology for automatic document organization. Within 20 minutes, the file is ready for download as an organized and bookmarked PDF file. In addition, the capital gains report is downloaded as an Autoflow document that will populate the tax return. This process also generates an Excel file with the required detail and is imported into the tax return.

- The tax return documents are left on the portal for three years and are then removed. Internally, the firm retains the records for eight years. Clients are responsible for setting up access to portal.

Benefits Achieved

- Most clients "love the portal, but some simply don't want it, and they prefer paper." Well over 50 percent of the clients are actively using the portal.
- No training on the portal is required for clients. Most clients just pick it up intuitively.
- Invoices are uploaded to the portal for three months, and the result has been a "positive impact on cash flow."
- Clients in other countries use the portal to upload their credit card information or wire transfers because of the security the portal provides for transmission and storage.

Lessons Learned

- ProFx Engagement works well as a document management system for all tax return engagements.
- Some have struggles remembering their portal password.
- The firm has explained to the clients their responsibilities for securing the portal.
- The TIFF file format offers a higher quality resolution for document recognition in Autoflow.
- The firm has set up their website to accept client payments using PayPal. However, this has had limited use at this point.

Krueger & Associates, P.A.: Leveraging a Cloud-Based Client Accounting Solution and Other Portal Applications

Firm Profile: Krueger & Associates, P.A., Tampa, Florida

Managing Partner: Kevin B. Krueger

Offices: 1

Partners: 1

Staff Size: 5 full-time, 1 part-time, 1–2 outside consultants

Services: Traditional services including 4–5 audits, numerous reviews and compilations, 550 individual returns, 500 entity returns.

Software Platform(s): Switched to CCH (software as a service [SaaS]): Practice, Workstream, Document, and Portal. Currently, 500 client portal accounts have been established.

Background: The cloud has allowed the firm to service clients throughout Tennessee, Georgia, and North Carolina from their office in Florida. They even have international clients in Thailand and Australia. The client in Thailand previously mailed tax returns that took over three months to receive. The portal has allowed them to eliminate the post office completely. Upon receiving e-mail permission from clients, the banker is set up for direct access to the portal for a period of five days, or permanently, based on the client/banker relationship.

Kreuger & Associates is fully embracing the cloud model with an innovative client service offering that includes Intacct, a true Web-based client accounting solution and Bill.com, a SaaS application for uploading client bills for processing and payment. For those clients who use Intacct as their accounting system, the firm can directly access the client's information anytime, anywhere. This eliminates a number of issues with the traditional model of gathering the client's general ledger files for import or reentry. The Intacct model allows the firm to provide their clients with a better solution by eliminating the process of exchanging the client's data files back and forth. With Bill.com, the firm's clients are able to e-mail or fax their invoices. Bill.com will upload the invoices to their account and process an Automated Clearing House (ACH) transaction to pay the bills. On a daily basis, the Bill.com transaction file posts directly into Intacct.

Benefits Achieved

- After finishing quarterly bonding covenants, the appropriate parties get an automatic e-mail letting them know that the file is available in the portal. In one example, the previous process required e-mailing 120 documents for 2 partners, 3 companies, and 5 banks.
- Eliminated all the issues associated with zip files and firewalls.
- Some older clients like the portal the best.
- Thirty-minute turnaround times to get feedback from clients to e-file. This gives clients the opportunity to review tax returns beforehand.
- One client said it (portal) "was the coolest thing she had ever seen."
- A banker called for a client's seven entities tax returns and was able to download them all within five minutes.
- They are able to drill down from the financial statement all the way down to the scanned source document.

Lessons Learned

- "Migration to the cloud is a process."
- Requires a business class Internet connection, preferably with a dedicated router and fiber optics. Procure the best and fastest backbone possible. The Internet connection is everything. Make sure you have the right service with backup.

- Procure two Internet connections for back-up purposes and configure for automatic cutover if primary service goes out.
- All staff connect from home, and everyone has the exact same setup with computers and multiple monitors. They use GoToMyPC to connect to their PC in the office.
- CCH SaaS applications perform faster than the traditional on-premise applications.
- Foundation side was not as fast because SaaS is better. Tremendously met with acceptance.
- Make sure the PC hardware and Operating System (OS) memory is as high as you can get. Don't let these be an impediment.
- Everyone has multiple monitors. They also use matrix video cards and have never any issues.
- With Intacct, Kreuger & Associates can provide clients with backup if their bookkeeper is out sick.
- The firm's Intacct fees are passed through to the client without markup, and they are charged hourly for services. The result is they receive higher fees from Intacct clients compared to bookkeeping clients. One client writes 1,200 checks per month with Intacct.
- Traditional write-up model is a "dinosaur" compared to the Intacct model.
- When you take the time to set up an application correctly, you don't have to go back and fix it.

Schlabig & Associates Ltd.: Outsourcing IT Infrastructure to a Data Center Hosting Service

Firm Profile: Schlabig & Associates Ltd., Akron & Kent, Ohio

Managing Partner: Thomas R. Hager

Firm Administrator: Kelly Nizzer Bates

Offices: 2

Partners: 3

Staff Size: 20

Services: Assurance, tax, succession planning, valuations, trust and estate plans, QuickBooks implementation and support.

Software Platform(s): Primarily Thomson-Reuters CS suite of accounting and tax software. The firm also uses Gruntworx from Copanion for organizing 1040 supporting documents.

Background: The firm used a traditional approach to IT up until 2007. This included an on-premise infrastructure with multiple servers and a dedicated internal IT professional to manage the systems. After trying a transition to a local IT managed services company in 2007, which was described as a "disaster," the firm made a strategic decision to outsource 100 percent of its IT services to Xcentric, LLC (www.xcentric.com).

Xcentric hosts the firm's file server infrastructure at its remote data center in Atlanta, Georgia. Both of the Schlabig offices connect to the server via T1 line (Akron Office) and AT&T U-Verse (Kent office). Both offices have a DSL service for backup. Upgrading the Kent office to a T1 line is planned in the near future.

The transition process went like this: The contract was signed in early September, and the firm went live during the first week in November. Once the contract was signed, a high level engineer was assigned to the firm. There was a weekly communication that took place to identify unknown issues, transfer of licenses, software, and so forth. Xcentric did all the research with the vendor and software companies directly and limited the firm's involvement in this step. At "go live," there was one full day of down time. The only training required was a 45-minute orientation in the firm's conference room to show what the new log-in procedures were. Because the applications were all the same as before, there was no additional training required. The staff was then asked to work as they normally would and report any issues in an online support ticket. Certain issues had to be resolved, such as a missing printer driver, a particular software application not showing up, and so forth.

Benefits Achieved

- Eliminated internal IT position and all associated costs. Firm administrator manages the Xcentric relationship.
- Partner time spent dealing with IT issues was reduced from the 5 percent to 8 percent range down to less than 1 percent, and all that time is focused on strategic issues. Similar benefits for the firm administrator with time spent on IT reduced from 30 percent to 35percent down to 5 percent to 8 percent, all focused on strategic issues as well.
- "Down time" went from frequent occurrences with on-premise infrastructure to virtually zero over the past four years, with a couple of minor outages.
- Achieved 100 percent anytime, anywhere access to all applications, data files, and digital documents.
- All software updates are now handled by Xcentric, and their knowledge of the accounting and tax industry is invaluable in helping to deal with software vendors and for offering IT best practices. All updates are processed after normal working hours for the firm to minimize disruption of the staff during the workdays.
- Absolutely no applications or firm data are installed on local PCs and laptops. Therefore, all personal and confidential information is maintained on the file servers at Xcentric's secure data center. All the data is also replicated and stored at a separate data center for better disaster recovery protection.
- The firm was able to transition from inconsistent processes between the two offices to a single standard for both offices.

Lessons Learned

- After a short stint with a local managed service provider, it became clear that industry expertise is a key to success, and the firm found that with Xcentric.
- Communication is critical. A ticketing system is used whereby support issues are prioritized. General tickets are cleared within a few hours depending on the urgency and the time of year. Identifying your time frame is critical to getting the response you need and requires that you be judicious in classifying what are truly "urgent" matters. There are times of the year when Xcentric is short on staff availability and, therefore, specific experts may not be immediately available.
- The Xcentric model offers a unique service with its ability to host 100 percent of the firm's applications. None of the software vendors can provide that single source solution.

Other Thoughts to Share

- The firm is utilizing the Gruntworx 1040 document organizer system. This is a software as a service application that converts an unorganized PDF of 1040 source documents and performs document recognition to place the documents in a logical sequence and create bookmarks automatically. Currently, the firm is using this as a back endscanning solution and is piloting a front end scanning workflow in 2012.
- The firm's staff has multiple monitors, and some of them have as many as four.
- Purchasing new hardware is simplified by using the Xcentric Store. Equipment is shipped to Xcentric for setup. After the firm receives the product, it takes an average of 15 minutes to set up and configure locally.

Appendix A

Sample Tax Services Process Review

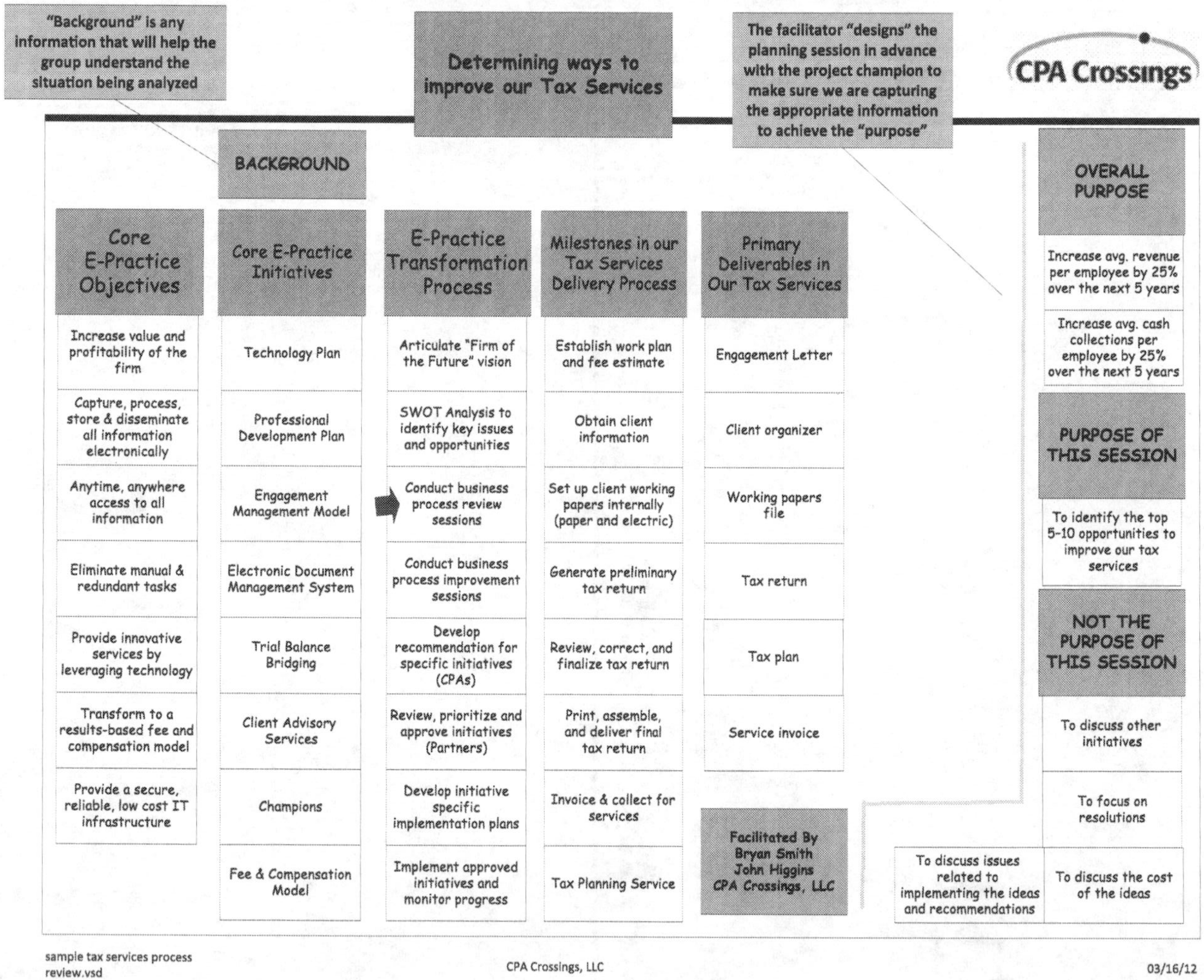
"Background" is any information that will help the group understand the situation being analyzed
Determining ways to improve our Tax Services
The facilitator "designs" the planning session in advance with the project champion to make sure we are capturing the appropriate information to achieve the "purpose"
CPA Crossings
BACKGROUND
Core E-Practice Objectives
Increase value and profitability of the firm
Capture, process, store & disseminate all information electronically
Anytime, anywhere access to all information
Eliminate manual & redundant tasks
Provide innovative services by leveraging technology
Transform to a results-based fee and compensation model
Provide a secure, reliable, low cost IT infrastructure
Core E-Practice Initiatives
Technology Plan
Professional Development Plan
Engagement Management Model
Electronic Document Management System
Trial Balance Bridging
Client Advisory Services
Champions
Fee & Compensation Model
E-Practice Transformation Process
Articulate "Firm of the Future" vision
SWOT Analysis to identify key issues and opportunities
Conduct business process review sessions
Conduct business process improvement sessions
Develop recommendation for specific initiatives (CPAs)
Review, prioritize and approve initiatives (Partners)
Develop initiative specific implementation plans
Implement approved initiatives and monitor progress
Milestones in our Tax Services Delivery Process
Establish work plan and fee estimate
Obtain client information
Set up client working papers internally (paper and electric)
Generate preliminary tax return
Review, correct, and finalize tax return
Print, assemble, and deliver final tax return
Invoice & collect for services
Tax Planning Service
Primary Deliverables in Our Tax Services
Engagement Letter
Client organizer
Working papers file
Tax return
Tax plan
Service invoice
Facilitated By
Bryan Smith
John Higgins
CPA Crossings, LLC
OVERALL PURPOSE
Increase avg. revenue per employee by 25% over the next 5 years
Increase avg. cash collections per employee by 25% over the next 5 years
PURPOSE OF THIS SESSION
To identify the top 5-10 opportunities to improve our tax services
NOT THE PURPOSE OF THIS SESSION
To discuss other initiatives
To focus on resolutions
To discuss issues related to implementing the ideas and recommendations
To discuss the cost of the ideas
sample tax services process review.vsd
CPA Crossings, LLC
03/16/12

CPA Crossings

Explore

Note that the approach used was to analyze the tax process to identify where there were opportunities to improve it. The IT issues to address were a byproduct of the process, not the primary focus

These are all the thoughts that were captured in the group brainstorming session. The participants where given a set of eight yellow dots to identify what items to focus on.

○ = the items that are the most important to focus on improving

Key steps in the tax process

- Mail Out Organizer for 1040's
- Request information from client for 1120's
- We identify likely clients, send out E.L. & Electronic pro forma is rolled
- Clients have option to access their pro forma via the web (currently ≈ 20%)
- Most clients mail back organizer, some come in for interview
- 50% mail back incomplete organizer with source documents
- Most 1120 clients are still sending in TB on computer printout
- We are starting to get some 1120 trial balances in electronic format

- Reviewer's initials are on return envelope. When they are received, scheduler is notified for scheduling 1040's
- 1120 returns are scheduled on a monthly basis
- Once scheduler assigns 1040's, the info is given to the preparer
- 1120 - The preparer works with the client to get the info. (sometimes via fieldwork)
- Corporate - We print a review copy. Preparer reviews and forward to reviewer (some reviewed online)
- 1040's - Reviewed on screen unless it is a complex return
- Tax file is delivered to reviewer for review

- Reviewer will correct 1040's & send forward, 1120 errors are sent back for correction
- Routing sheet travels w/ tax file
- Final print 1) client 2) Firm file 3) IRS (ex. e-file)
- Option for client review via e-mail if so desired
- Printed copies are returned to reviewer, then to assistant to assemble and mail or return for signature
- We return source documents to clients
- Some source documents are copied for firm file - most are returned
- Some clients prefer to have firm store source documents

- Most returns are billed on monthly WIP cycle
- Fees are based on time x rate (prior years used as a benchmark est.)
- Primarily deal w/ billing issues at the time of billing
- 480-1040's and 100 extensions + 20 extensions
- 150 - 200 Business returns
- We don't commit to a turn around date

Tools used in the tax process

- Pro Systems & ProFx for all returns
- Perform Plus to generate tax forms for manual completion
- BNA Planning software for individual & corporate tax planning
- Depreciation is done in ProFx or CSI's Depreciation Solutions
- Depreciation Solutions produces depreciation tax form - totals entered in ProFx
- Tax tools for p/r forms, amort. Schedules, lots of other utilities
- PPT software - Tax Time
- CCH & BNA research online (web based)

- Mutual fund tax info. Com dividend information / tax status
- Reference books; deprec., Master Tax Guide (paper & electronic)
- Excel
- Various web sites
- AuditVision for linking corporate TB's
- Tax due list (1120's) is maintained in Access

Documents & reports used in the tax process

- Routing Sheet
- Request for research form (not used)
- Pro formas for gathering client data
- Organizers (printed internally)
- Most tax returns are delivered with two years' comparison
- Some clients receive envelopes for mailing tax returns
- E-file clients get everything except a paper IRS copy
- BNA generates a planning report

- E.L. generated by Pro System
- Majority of E.L.s don't get signed. Corporate are usually signed
- Organizer form has prior year info for client review
- Checklist w/ suggestions for preparing returns (part of 1040 route sheet)
- Client interview questionairre on organizer
- AICPA financial planning CD w/ checklists, tables, sample E.L., etc.
- Various Excel templates that get used for calculations

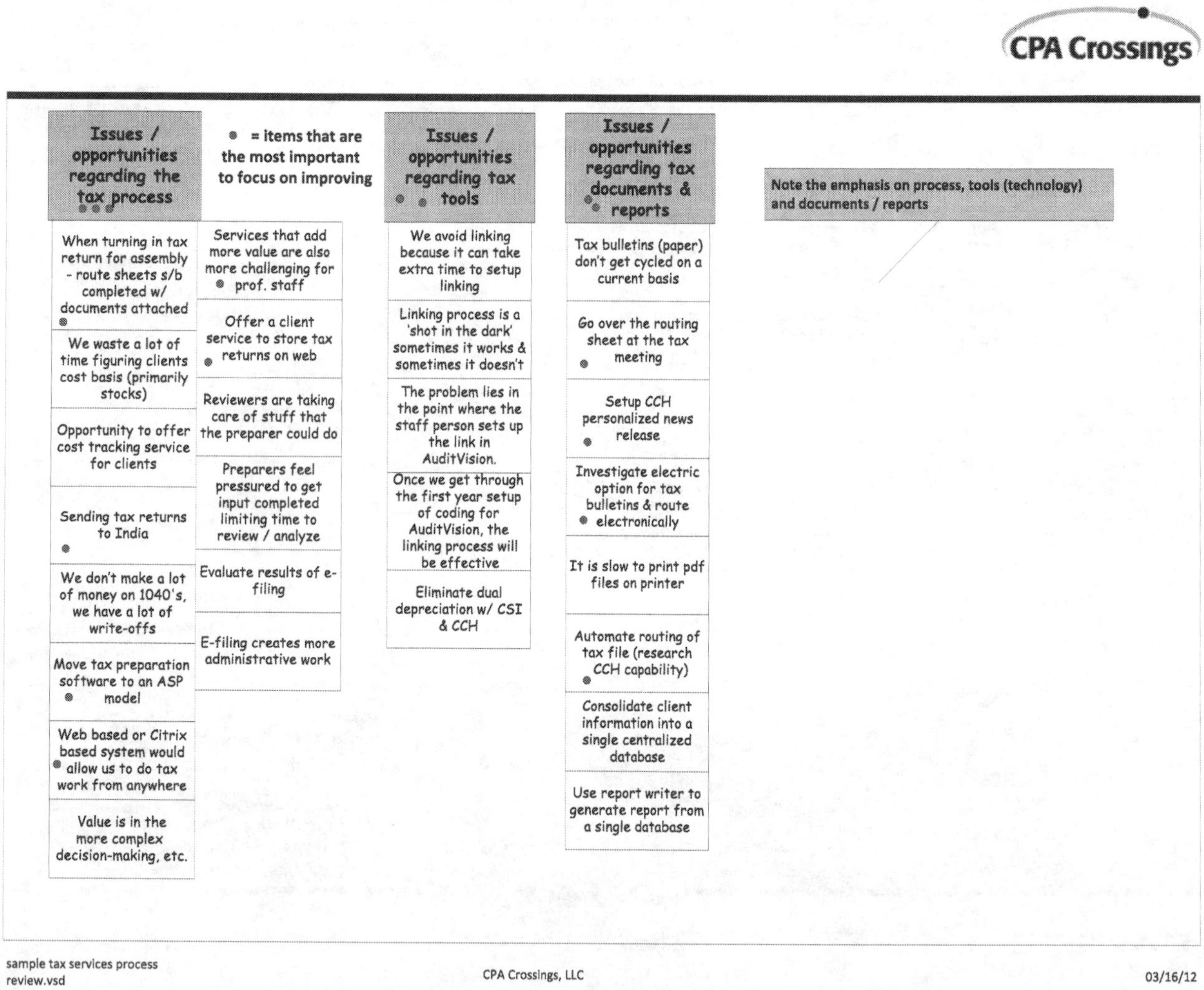
CPA Crossings
Issues / opportunities regarding the tax process
● = items that are the most important to focus on improving
Issues / opportunities regarding tax tools
Issues / opportunities regarding tax documents & reports
Note the emphasis on process, tools (technology) and documents / reports
When turning in tax return for assembly - route sheets s/b completed w/ documents attached
We waste a lot of time figuring clients cost basis (primarily stocks)
Opportunity to offer cost tracking service for clients
Sending tax returns to India
We don't make a lot of money on 1040's, we have a lot of write-offs
Move tax preparation software to an ASP model
Web based or Citrix based system would allow us to do tax work from anywhere
Value is in the more complex decision-making, etc.
Services that add more value are also more challenging for prof. staff
Offer a client service to store tax returns on web
Reviewers are taking care of stuff that the preparer could do
Preparers feel pressured to get input completed limiting time to review / analyze
Evaluate results of e-filing
E-filing creates more administrative work
We avoid linking because it can take extra time to setup linking
Linking process is a 'shot in the dark' sometimes it works & sometimes it doesn't
The problem lies in the point where the staff person sets up the link in AuditVision.
Once we get through the first year setup of coding for AuditVision, the linking process will be effective
Eliminate dual depreciation w/ CSI & CCH
Tax bulletins (paper) don't get cycled on a current basis
Go over the routing sheet at the tax meeting
Setup CCH personalized news release
Investigate electric option for tax bulletins & route electronically
It is slow to print pdf files on printer
Automate routing of tax file (research CCH capability)
Consolidate client information into a single centralized database
Use report writer to generate report from a single database
sample tax services process review.vsd
CPA Crossings, LLC
03/16/12

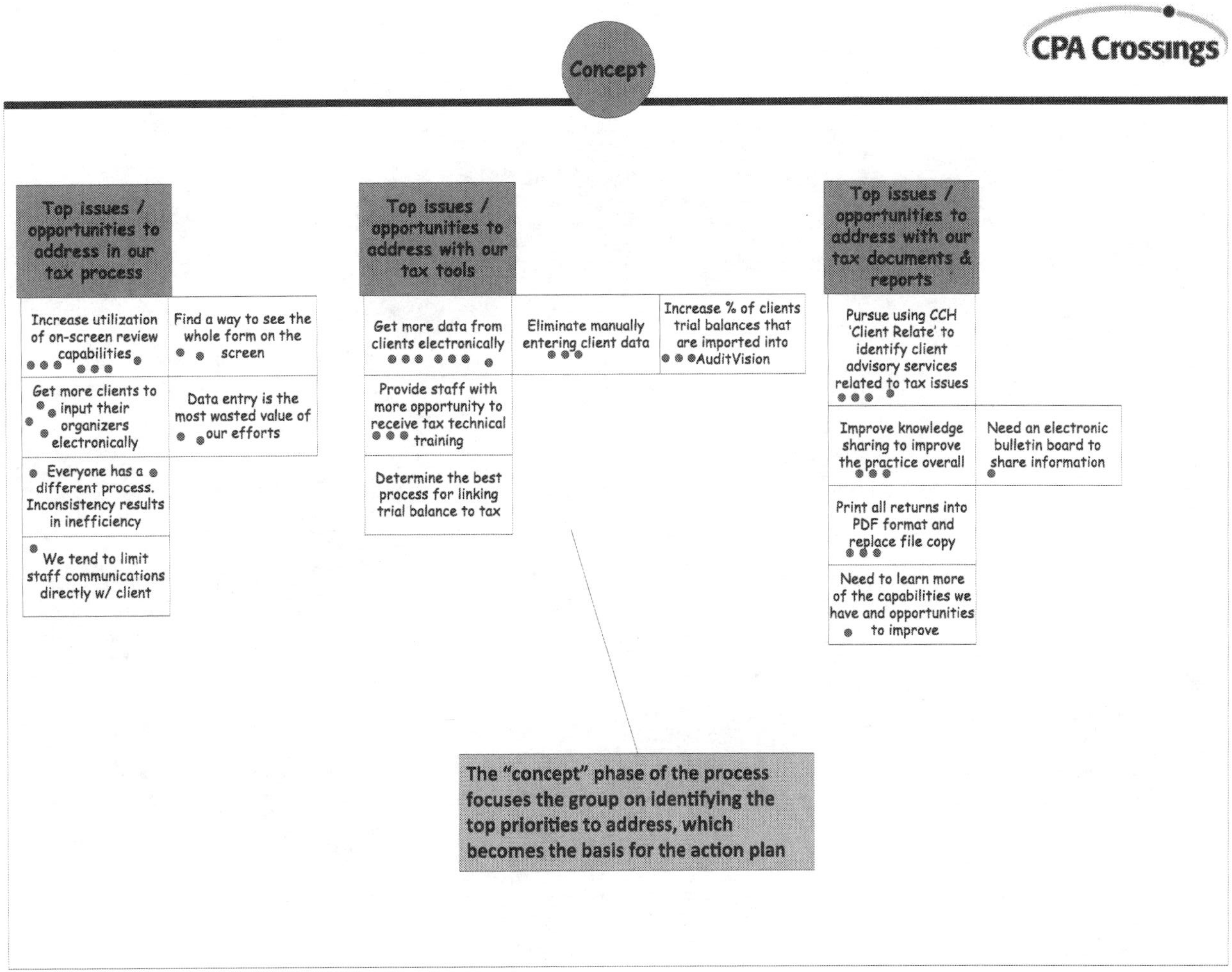

sample tax services process review.vsd

CPA Crossings, LLC

03/16/12

CPA Crossings

Action Plan

TASKS	WHO WILL DO IT	DEADLINE
Document results of this session	CPAs	5/15
Distribute to participants	CPAs	5/17
Integrate results into initiative implementation planning	CPAs	TBD

Every planning session includes the development of either a macro- or micro-level action plan in order to move the initiative to the next steps.

sample tax services process review.vsd

CPA Crossings, LLC

03/16/12

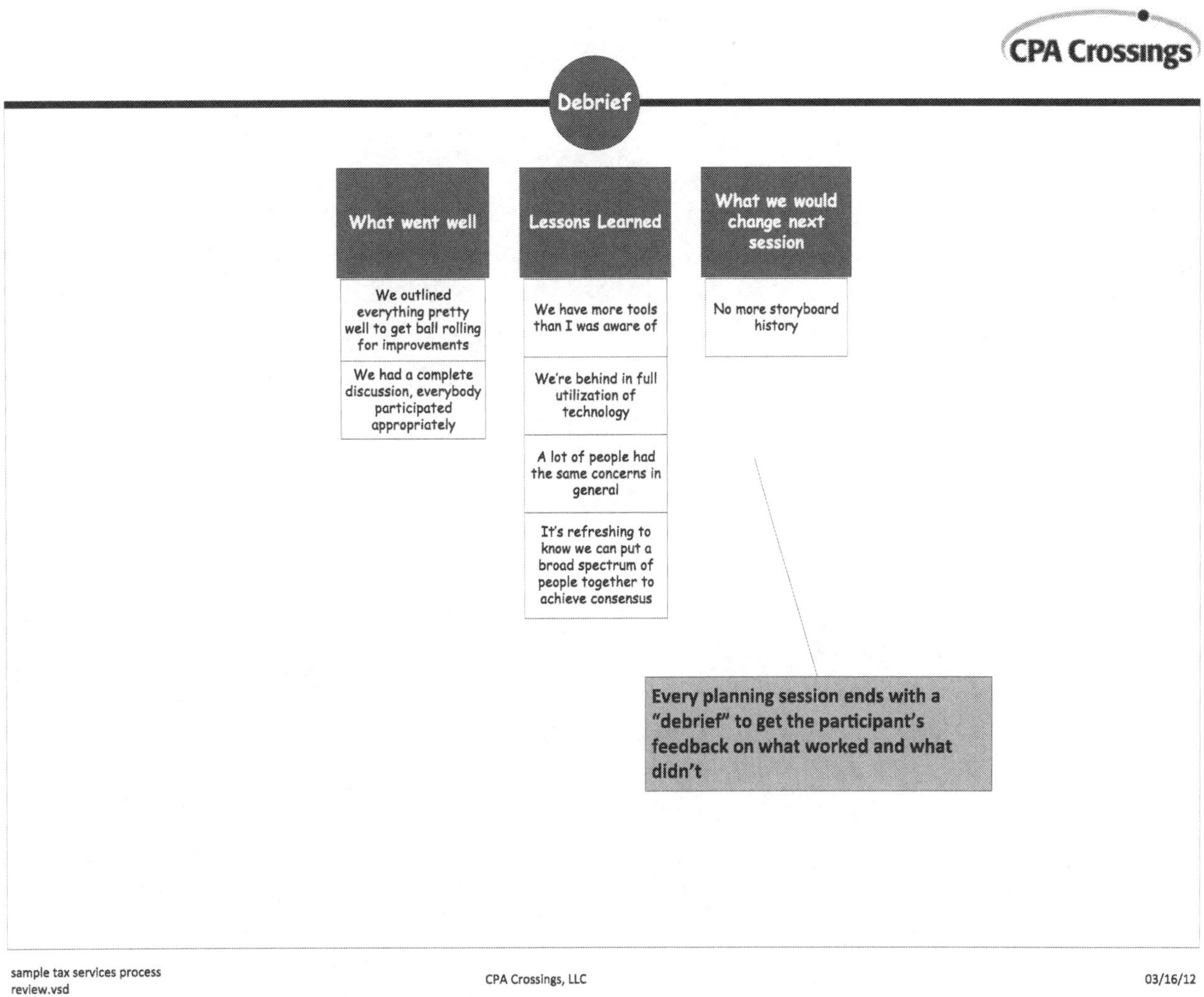
CPA Crossings
Debrief
What went well
We outlined everything pretty well to get ball rolling for improvements
We had a complete discussion, everybody participated appropriately
Lessons Learned
We have more tools than I was aware of
We're behind in full utilization of technology
A lot of people had the same concerns in general
It's refreshing to know we can put a broad spectrum of people together to achieve consensus
What we would change next session
No more storyboard history
Every planning session ends with a "debrief" to get the participant's feedback on what worked and what didn't
sample tax services process review.vsd
CPA Crossings, LLC
03/16/12

Appendix B

Glossary of Cloud Computing Terms Related to Client Accounting Service Delivery

back-office processes. Supporting business functions, such as accounting, finance, payroll, employee benefits, and IT that provide infrastructure for an organization's vision and create a platform for growth. Back-office processes are also referred to as *noncore processes*.

business process outsourcing. A process of delegating the back-office processes or noncore business functions to a third party service provider.

client accounting services. Services offered by CPA firms to their clients to help them manage their finance and accounting functions. Although the services offered within a client accounting services practice vary, they generally fall into three categories: (1) after-the-fact financial statement preparation, (2) transaction processing, and (3) CFO/controller services.

client assessment. A thorough review of a client's current operating environment to gain insight into his or her current business operations. This includes reviewing and documenting operational workflow and business practices, understanding and documenting business structure, and control activity information. This information enables the CPA firm to understand areas of the client's operation that can be improved and how your firm's services and systems can address those areas for improvement.

client service delivery model. This describes the methodology a CPA firm uses to share software and data when performing client accounting services. There are generally three service delivery models:

1. Where the software resides at the client's location and at the firm's location; the software may or may not be the same. The firm and client exchange data files. Soft copies of the file may be exchanged in various ways.
2. Where the software and data resides on third party software as a service (SaaS) cloud-based (or Web-based) servers. Both the client and firm share this common cloud-based business platform. Client and firm access the software and data via an Internet browser.
3. A combination of the both options.

cloud-based computing. The term *cloud* is used as a metaphor for the Internet. Typical cloud computing service providers deliver common business applications and software online, which are accessed from a Web browser, while the software and data are stored on third party servers. Clients can typically purchase access as needed and can increase or reduce services as their needs change. The cloud computing service delivery vendor develops and supports the solution and runs all operations.

core business processes. These are the business processes that move an organization's vision forward, such as sales, marketing, business development, and customer service. Core business processes are also referred to as *front-office processes.*

field examination and discovery. A part of the client assessment process that involves being on-site at the client's operations, meeting with business process owners, and studying the current operations and workflow.

finance and accounting outsourcing (FAO). A specific type of outsourcing known as FAO for *finance and accounting outsourcing* or *the outsourcing of an organization's finance and accounting* (F&A) *functions.* This is a term used by companies to describe the outsourcing of their F&A function. It is also used by accounting firms to describe services they provide.

front-office processes. These are the business functions that move an organization's vision forward, such as sales, marketing, business development, and customer service. Front-office processes are also referred to as *core business processes.*

hosting. This is a software deployment in which the customer acquires the software, and a service provider delivers IT infrastructure and "hosts" by creating a single operating environment (virtual or physical) to allow a single customer to access and utilize dedicated computing resources for a software vendor's product.

A few points to consider:

- These applications are traditional, single-tenant applications but hosted by a third party. They are client-server applications with HTML front ends added to allow remote access to the application.

- The applications are not written as net-native applications. As a result, the performance and application updates may be no better than self-managed premise-based applications.

By comparison, cloud-based SaaS applications are multitenant applications hosted by a vendor that have been designed as net-native applications that automatically get updated on an ongoing basis.

on-demand service. Services delivered in which a client can purchase access to software delivered via the Internet. Clients can purchase access as needed and can increase or reduce services as their needs change. Also known as *software as a service.*

scalability. The measure of a service's ability to increase or decrease in performance and cost in response to changes in needs or volume. It is important that a service be scalable if an organization anticipates growth and increased needs.

service delivery platform. The software solutions and technology components that will be used in a firm's client accounting service delivery.

service organization or provider. Within the context of cloud computing, the service organization or provider is the business that delivers a cloud computing application as a service for a monthly fee.

service level agreement (SLA). A contractual agreement in which a service provider defines the level of service, responsibilities, priorities, and guarantees regarding timing, availability, performance, and other aspects of the service.

service level requirements (SLR). A document in which the business requirements for outsourced services are recorded. The SLR provides a basis for negotiations linked to the formulation of SLAs.

software as a service (SaaS). Cloud application services in which applications are delivered over the Internet by the software provider, typically for a monthly fixed fee. The applications are not installed, nor do they run on the client's computers; instead, they are accessed by a Web browser. Two important characteristics of SaaS are as follows:

- Network and Web-based access to commercial software computing services in which the processing is done on a third party server, rather than at each customer's location.
- A tenant-based pricing model for hardware, software, administration, and consulting services.

Appendix C

Resource Center

I. Chapter 3: Infrastructure

   A. Hosting and Managed Services

      1. CPA ASP – A hosting provider for accounting and financial software, including QuickBooks, MAS90, Macola, Peachtree, Thomson Reuters CS Accounting, Act!, Goldmine, ProSystems fx, Ultratax, Drake Tax, Lacerte, and more.
         www.cpaasp.com
      2. NMGI – Provides comprehensive proactive management, maintenance, and troubleshooting for all your IT assets (servers, desktops, firewalls, routers, switches, and other devices).
         www.nmgi.com
      3. Xcentric – CPA firm focused hosting organization that hosts 1,000+ applications for firms nationwide.
         www.xcentric.com

   B. Remote Access

      1. GoToMyPC – Citrix-owned organization that provides remote access via the Internet to most operating systems and platforms.
         http://www.gotomypc.com/remote_access/remote_access

2. LogMeIn – Use LogMeIn to remotely support, manage, and back up hundreds or thousands of desktops, laptops, servers, kiosks, point of service/sale (POS) machines, and the applications that run on them.
   www.logmein.com
3. Microsoft Remote Desktop Connection – Included in most Windows operating systems.
   http://windows.microsoft.com/en-US/windows-vista/Remote-Desktop-Connection-frequently-asked-questions

II. Chapter 4: Bandwidth
   A. AT&T – National provider of various Internet solutions.
      www.att.com/Common/storefront/reco/index.html
   B. CenturyLink – Now includes Qwest to provide a larger national presence.
      www.centurylink.com/small-business/products/business-solutions/
   C. Charter – Regional cable Internet provider.
      www.charterbusiness.com
   D. Comcast – Regional cable Internet provider.
      http://business.comcast.com/smb2
   E. Time Warner Cable – Regional cable Internet provider.
      www.twcbc.com
   F. TW Telecom – Regional Internet provider.
      www.twtelecom.com
   G. Verizon – National provider of various Internet solutions.
      http://smallbusiness.verizon.com
      www.verizonbusiness.com/Medium/
   H. XO Communications – Regional Internet provider.
      http://smallbusiness.xo.com/
      www.xo.com/solutions/business/Pages/medium-business.aspx
   I. Utilities
      1. SpeedTests – Use these sites to test your Internet speed, including download and upload speeds.
         www.speedtest.net
         www.speakeasy.net/speedtest/

III. Chapter 5: The CPA Technology Toolkit
   A. Adobe Acrobat
      1. Version comparison – A detailed comparison of the features of the various Adobe Acrobat versions.
         www.adobe.com/products/acrobatpro/buying-guide.html?promoid=JIJYS
   B. Adobe TV – Online video resource for expert instruction and inspiration about Adobe products.
      http://tv.adobe.com/

C. Microsoft
   1. Office
      a. General information, help, templates, and more – A starting point to find learning resources for Microsoft Office.
         http://office.microsoft.com/en-us/
      b. Version comparison – Provides a comparison of the various Office versions.
         http://office.microsoft.com/en-us/buy/office-2010-which-suite-is-right-for-you-FX101825640.aspx
      c. Volume licensing – Resources to learn about saving money when more than five Office licenses are needed.
         http://office.microsoft.com/en-us/buy/office-2010-volume-licensing-suites-comparison-FX101825637.aspx
      d. Microsoft License Advisor – Provides an interface to calculate the cost of volume licensing fees.
         www.microsoft.com/licensing/mla/
      e. Office 365 Pricing Plans – Learn what is included in the various Office 365 plans and the per user cost.
         www.microsoft.com/en-us/office365/all-plans.aspx#fbid=HAaavF47heg
   2. Windows
      a. General information, help, how-to, and more – A starting point to find learning resources for Microsoft Windows.
         http://windows.microsoft.com/en-US/windows7/products/home
      b. Version comparison – Provides a comparison of the various Windows versions.
         http://windows.microsoft.com/en-US/windows7/products/compare

D. Google Apps
   1. General information – Learn about Google Apps.
      www.google.com/apps/intl/en/business/index.html
   2. Pricing and features – Provides pricing and feature information.
      www.google.com/apps/intl/en/business/features.html
   3. Version comparison – Provides a comparison of the various Google Apps versions.
      www.google.com/apps/intl/en/index.html

E. E-mail
   1. Hosting
      a. Apptix – AICPA Trusted Business Advisor Solutions provider.
         www.apptix.com/retail/cpa2bizemail/index.html
      b. CPA.com – AICPA Trusted Business Advisor Solutions provider.
         http://clientsolutions.cpa2biz.com/CPA/Index.html
      c. Microsoft
         i. General information – Learn about Microsoft's Exchange hosting solution.
            www.microsoft.com/exchange/en-us/exchange-online-hosted-email.aspx

   ii. Comparison with Google Apps – Provides a comparison between Microsoft's and Google's hosting solutions.
   www.microsoft.com/exchange/en-us/google-apps.aspx

F. Web Conferencing
   1. Adobe Connect – Web conferencing provided by Adobe.
      www.adobe.com/products/adobeconnect.html
   2. GoToMeeting – Web conferencing provided by Citrix.
      www.gotomeeting.com
   3. Microsoft Lync – Web conferencing provided by Microsoft.
      http://lync.microsoft.com
   4. WebEx – Web conferencing provided by Cisco.
      www.webex.com

G. Desktops and Laptops
   1. Dell
      www.dell.com/aicpa
   2. Hewlett Packard (HP)
      www.hp.com/go/aicpa
   3. Lenovo
      www.cpa2biz.com/AST/AICPA_CPA2BIZ_Browse/Member_Benefits/Programs/Lenovo.jsp
      http://shoplenovo.i2.com/SEUILibrary/controller/e/aicpagold/StdAffinityPortal/en_US/StdAffinity:Home?home=aicpagold&affinity=aicpagold

H. Monitors
   1. Dell
      www.dell.com/aicpa
   2. HP
      www.hp.com/go/aicpa
   3. Lenovo
      www.cpa2biz.com/AST/AICPA_CPA2BIZ_Browse/Member_Benefits/Programs/Lenovo.jsp
      http://shoplenovo.i2.com/SEUILibrary/controller/e/aicpagold/StdAffinityPortal/en_US/StdAffinity:Home?home=aicpagold&affinity=aicpagold
   4. Samsung
      www.samsung.com/us/computer/monitors
   5. View Sonic
      www.viewsonic.com/products/desktop-monitors/

I. Smartphones
   1. Carriers and Distributors
      a. Apple – Get the iPhone for any carrier directly from Apple.
         www.apple.com/iphone

   b. AT&T – National carrier of most smartphones.
      www.cpa2biz.com/AST/AICPA_CPA2BIZ_Browse/Member_Benefits/Programs/ATT.jsp?FOLDER%3C%3Efolder_id=1408474395181549&bmUID=1328651090621
      http://clk.atdmt.com/CNT/go/144221517/direct/01/
   c. Best Buy – Choose from a variety of smartphones with plans from AT&T, Sprint, T-Mobile, and Verizon.
      www.bestbuy.com
   d. Sprint – National carrier of most smartphones.
      www.sprint.com
   e. Verizon – National carrier of most smartphones.
      www.verizon.com
2. Phones
   a. Apple – Manufacturer of the iPhone.
      www.apple.com/iphone
   b. Research In Motion (RIM) – Manufacturer of the BlackBerry.
      www.blackberry.com
   c. HTC – Manufacturer of Android and Windows Mobile smartphones.
      www.htc.com
   d. Motorola – Manufacturer of Android smartphones.
      www.motorola.com/Consumers/US-EN/Home?WT.mc_id=CLP_Traffic&WT.mc_ev=click
   e. Samsung – Manufacturer of Android and Windows Mobile smartphones.
      www.samsung.com/us/mobile/cell-phones
3. AICPA Resources
   a. Mobile and Remote Computing
      www.aicpa.org/interestareas/informationtechnology/resources/cloud-computing/pages/default.aspx

J. Tablets
   1. Acer – Manufacturer of Android tablets.
      http://us.acer.com/ac/en/US/content/group/tablets
   2. Apple – Manufacturer of iPad tablets.
      www.apple.com
   3. BlackBerry – Manufacturer of Android tablets.
      http://us.blackberry.com/playbook-tablet/
   4. Dell – Manufacturer of Android tablets.
      www.dell.com/us/business/p/latitude-laptops?~ck=anav
   5. Lenovo – Manufacturer of Android tablets.
      www.lenovo.com/products/us/tablet/
   6. Motorola – Manufacturer of Android tablets.
      www.motorola.com/Consumers/US-EN/Consumer-Product-and-Services/Tablets

7. Samsung – Manufacturer of Android tablets.
   www.samsung.com/us/mobile/galaxy-tab
8. View Sonic – Manufacturer of Android and Windows tablets.
   www.viewsonic.com/products/tablets/view-all-models/

IV. Chapter 6: Scanning Solutions

A. Software for Scanning and Organizing

1. CCH – ProSystem fx Scan – A scanning product that sorts scanned documents into an organized PDF.
   www.cchgroup.com/prosystemscan
2. Drake Software – Gruntworx – A secure, Web-based application that automates the time-consuming tasks of gathering, organizing, and populating client tax data into tax preparation software.
   www.copanion.com
3. Kofax – VRS Elite – Software that automatically examines documents and applies the correct settings to deliver high quality scanned images.
   www.kofax.com/vrs-virtualrescan/
4. SurePrep – A cloud application to organize 1040 working papers and documents.
   http://corp.sureprep.com/
5. Thomson Reuters – Scanflow – Scans documents in bulk and organizes them with the highest degree of accuracy by leveraging barcode and optical character recognition (OCR) technology.
   http://cs.thomsonreuters.com/gofileroom/scanning.aspx

B. Hardware

1. Canon
   www.usa.canon.com/cusa/consumer/products/scanners/document_scanners
2. Fujitsu
   www.fujitsu.com/global/services/computing/peripheral/scanners/fi/lineup/
3. Xerox
   www.xeroxscanners.com/en/us/

V. Chapter 7: Document and File Management Systems

A. CabinetNG – A platform for document management and workflow automation to a wide business spectrum. Cloud or on-premise application.
   www.cabinetng.com

B. CCH – ProSystem fx Document – A document management system specifically designed for the CPA firm and integration with the ProSystem fx products. Cloud or on-premise application.
   www.cchgroup.com/prosystemdocument

C. Doc-It – A leading provider of practice-wide document management and archiving solutions. On-premise application.
   www.doc-it.com

D. Office Tools Pro
   www.officetoolspro.com

E. Thomson Reuters – FileCabinet CS – A document management system that operates like an electronic file cabinet with integration into the CS Professional Suite of products. Cloud or on-premise application.
http://cs.thomsonreuters.com/FileCabinetCS/

F. Thomson Reuters – GoFileRoom – A cloud-based document management application written to take advantage of Microsoft Internet Explorer with integration into FirmFlow and ClientFlow.
http://cs.thomsonreuters.com/gofileroom

VI. Chapter 8: Trial Balance Working Paper Software

A. CaseWare Working Papers – A highly flexible engagement software that provides you with everything you would expect from an assurance and reporting tool. Engagements are planned, performed, and reviewed entirely on screen, completely eliminating paper.
www.caseware.com/products/working-papers

B. CCH – ProSystem fx Engagement – An engagement management system specifically designed for the CPA firm and integration with the ProSystem fx products. Cloud or on-premise application.
www.cchgroup.com/prosystemengagement

C. Thomson Reuters – Engagement CS – A tax workflow and accounting audit management software that easily organizes any professional engagement, from planning and review to final document archiving, ensuring a complete, accurate, and cost-effective audit engagement every time. Cloud or on-premise application.
http://cs.thomsonreuters.com/engagement/

VII. Chapter 9: Client Portals—Gateway to the Future

A. CCH – ProSystem fx Portal – A client portal that integrates with the ProSystem fx products.
www.cchgroup.com/portal

B. CPA Site Solutions – An organization that provides client portals in addition to services to give any CPA firm a greater Internet presence.
www.cpasitesolutions.com

C. eMoney Advisors – A client portal for wealth management services.
http://www.emoneyadvisor.com/emacorp/products.aspx

D. Microsoft – SharePoint – A customizable portal for a multitude of portal needs.
http://sharepoint.microsoft.com

E. Thomson Reuters – NetClient CS – A client portal that integrates with the CS Professional Suite of products.
http://cs.thomsonreuters.com/portals/

VIII. Chapter 10: Workflow Software

A. AICPA – Interactive Tax Checklists – A cloud-based tax checklist system.
http://clientsolutions.cpa2biz.com/ITC/Index.html

B. CCH – Workstream – Workflow software that integrates with the ProSystem fx products.
http://tax.cchgroup.com/workstream

C. Thomson Reuters – FirmFlow – Workflow software that integrates with GoFileRoom.
http://cs.thomsonreuters.com/FirmFlow

D. XCM – An automated workflow solution for the accounting profession.
www.xcmsolutions.com

IX. Chapter 11: Cloud-Based Client Accounting System

A. AccountantsWorld – A variety of applications from write-up to client accounting.
www.accountantsworld.com

B. Bill.com – A low-cost, cloud-based bill management service that streamlines and automates your clients' accounts payable and receivable processes with complete security and control.
http://clientsolutions.cpa2biz.com/Paperless/index.html

C. Intacct – A cloud-based, on-demand financial management solution that helps you and your clients work smarter, faster, and more efficiently.
www.cpa2biz.com/AST/AICPA_CPA2BIZ_Browse/Member_Benefits/Programs/Intacct.jsp

D. Intuit – QuickBooks Online – Cloud-based version of QuickBooks.
www.quickbooksonline.com

E. NetSuite – An Oracle product with a wide variety of applications.
www.netsuite.com

F. Thomson Reuters – Client Bookkeeping Solutions – A simple accounting system that integrates with the CS Professional Suite of products.
http://cs.thomsonreuters.com/cs-accounting/client.aspx

G. Xero – A cloud-based accounting system with integration to many third party websites.
www.xero.com

X. Chapter 12: Security and Disaster Recovery

A. AICPA Resources

1. Security
www.aicpa.org/interestareas/informationtechnology/resources/information-securitymanagement/pages/informationsm.aspx

2. Disaster Recovery Planning
www.aicpa.org/interestareas/informationtechnology/resources/business continuitymanagementanddisasterrecoveryplanning/pages/default.aspx

a. Quick and Easy Business Continuity Plan for Your Small Business: Step-by-Step Template With Sample Plans on CD
www.cpa2biz.com/AST/Main/CPA2BIZ_Primary/PracticeManagement/PRDOVR~PC-991011/PC-991011.jsp

b. Principles and Practices of Business Continuity: Tools and Techniques
www.cpa2biz.com/AST/Main/CPA2BIZ_Primary/PracticeManagement/PRDOVR~PC-991012/PC-991012.jsp

B. Firewalls
   1. Barracuda
      www.barracudanetworks.com/ns/products/
   2. Check Point
      www.checkpoint.com
   3. Cisco
      www.cisco.com/en/US/products/ps5708/Products_Sub_Category_Home.html
   4. SonicWALL
      www.sonicwall.com/us/products/Network_Security_Appliances.html
   5. Watchguard
      www.watchguard.com/products/xtm-main.asp

C. Encryption
   1. Check Point
      www.checkpoint.com/products/full-disk-encryption/index.html
   2. PGP (Pretty Good Privacy)
      www.symantec.com/whole-disk-encryption
      www.symantec.com/content/en/us/enterprise/fact_sheets/b-pgp_desktop_email_DS_21158806.en-us.pdf
   3. List of Other Encryption Software
      http://en.wikipedia.org/wiki/Comparison_of_disk_encryption_software

D. Password Programs
   1. Kaspersky – Password Manager
      http://usa.kaspersky.com/products-services/home-computer-security/password-manager
   2. RoboForm
      www.roboform.com
   3. List of Other Password Programs
      http://password-management-software-review.toptenreviews.com/

E. Password Policies
   1. SANS Institute
      http://www.sans.org/security-resources/policies/Password_Policy.pdf

F. Malware Prevention
   1. Avast!
      www.avast.com
   2. AVG (Anti-Virus Guard)
      www.avg.com
   3. Kaspersky
      www.kaspersky.com
   4. Lookout Mobile Security
      www.mylookout.com

5. McAfee
   www.mcafee.com
6. Symantec
   www.symantec.com
7. Trend Micro
   www.trendmicro.com

G. Secure USB
1. IronKey and MXI Security (now owned by Imation Corp.)
   www.imation.com/en-US/Mobile-Security/Mobile-Security-Products/Secure-Mobile-Data-encrypted-USB-drives/
2. Kingston Technology
   www.kingston.com/us/usb/encrypted_security
3. List of Other Secure USB Drives
   http://secure-usb-drive-review.toptenreviews.com/

H. Online Backup
1. Carbonite
   www.carbonite.com
2. CPA.com Back-Up Solutions
   http://clientsolutions.cpa2biz.com/Backup/index.html
3. Mozy
   www.mozy.com
4. OpenDrive
   www.opendrive.com
5. SugarSync
   www.sugarsync.com
6. List of Other Online Backup Solutions
   http://online-data-backup-review.toptenreviews.com/

XI. Help and How To Resources

A. AICPA – CPA2BIZ
   www.cpa2biz.com

B. AICPA – Glossary of Cloud Computing Terms Related to Client Accounting Service Delivery
   http://clientsolutions.cpa2biz.com/Practice/Documents/Glossary.pdf

C. CPA Practice Advisors – A resource that focuses on the need for the CPA practice.
   www.cpapracticeadvisor.com

D. McNellis Compression Planning – A structured process for all your planning needs.
   www.mcnellisco.com

E. MSDN (Microsoft Developer Network) – Microsoft's technical support website.
   http://msdn.microsoft.com

F. Tech Republic – A resource for any information technology need.
   www.techrepublic.com

G. XBRL – eXtensible Business Reporting Language (XBRL) is a language for the electronic communication of business and financial data that is set to revolutionize business reporting around the world.
www.aicpa.org/InterestAreas/CenterForAuditQuality/Resources/CAQAudit Library/Pages/XBRL.aspx

XII. AICPA SOC (Service Organization Controls) References and Resources | The AICPA has developed a comprehensive library of resources to assist practitioners in the assessment and evaluation of outsourced service providers, for example, cloud computing service providers.

A. SOC Reports Information for Service Organizations
B. SOC Reports Information for CPAs
C. Service Organization Control (SOC) Reports
D. SOC Reports Member Toolkit
E. SOC 1
F. Comparison of SOC 1, SOC 2, and SOC 3 Reports
G. AICPA SOC products:

1. *Service Organizations: Applying SSAE No. 16,* Reporting on Controls at a Service Organization(SOC 1) – This guide is designed to assist CPAs in transitioning from performing a service auditor's engagement under Statement on Auditing Standards (SAS) No. 70, *Service Organizations*, to doing so under Statement on Standards for Attestation Engagements (SSAE) No. 16, *Reporting on Controls at a Service Organization*, which replaces the guidance for service auditors in SAS No. 70.
www.cpa2biz.com/AST/Main/CPA2BIZ_Primary/AuditAttest/Industry-specificGuidance/PRDOVR~PC-0127910/PC-0127910.jsp
2. Service Organization Control Reports SM: SOC 1, SOC 2, and SOC 3 On-Demand Series – This series of courses will provide information and guidance on the three new reporting options on controls at a service organization that have replaced SAS 70 reports.
www.cpa2biz.com/AST/Main/CPA2BIZ_Primary/AuditAttest/PRDOVR~PC-780281/PC-780281.jsp
3. *Reporting on Controls at a Service Organization Relevant to Security, Availability, Processing Integrity, Confidentiality, or Privacy* (SOC 2) – This new guide summarizes the three new service organization controls engagements and provides detailed guidance for performing examinations under AT section 101, *Attest Engagements* (AICPA, *Professional Standards*), to report on a service organization's controls over its system relevant to security, availability, processing integrity, confidentiality, or privacy, commonly referred to as a SOC 2 engagement.
www.cpa2biz.com/AST/Main/CPA2BIZ_Primary/AuditAttest/Industry-specificGuidance/PRDOVR~PC-0128210/PC-0128210.jsp
4. *Service Organizations: New Reporting Options* – This alert provides information on a recently issued SSAE and a finalized SAS.
www.cpa2biz.com/AST/Main/CPA2BIZ_Primary/AuditAttest/Industry-specificGuidance/PRDOVR~PC-0224811/PC-0224811.jsp

Appendix D

AICPA SOC References and Resources

Service Organization Control Reports

(www.aicpa.org/interestareas/frc/assuranceadvisoryservices/pages/sorhome.aspx)

Overview: Service Organization Control (SOC) reports are internal control reports on the services provided by a service organization providing valuable information that users need to assess and address the risks associated with an outsourced service.

SOC Reports Information for Service Organizations

(www.aicpa.org/interestareas/frc/assuranceadvisoryservices/pages/serviceorganization's management.aspx)

Overview: SOC reports are designed to help service organizations, which are organizations that operate information systems and provide information system services to other entities, build trust and confidence in their service delivery processes and controls through a report by an independent CPA. Each type of SOC report is designed to help service organizations meet specific user needs.

SOC Reports Information for CPAs

(www.aicpa.org/interestareas/frc/assuranceadvisoryservices/pages/cpas.aspx)

Overview: To make CPAs aware of the various standards available to them for examining and reporting on controls at a service organization and to help CPAs select the appropriate standard for a particular engagement, the AICPA has introduced Service Organization Control SM Reports and identified 3 different engagements (SOC 1, SOC 2, and SOC 3) that involve reporting on controls at a service organization. The following table identifies features of each of these engagements.

SOC Reports Member Toolkit

(www.aicpa.org/interestareas/frc/assuranceadvisoryservices/pages/socreportsmembertoolkit.aspx)

Tools: The AICPA developed resources to help CPAs explain the new series of SOC reports to current and potential clients and for firms to market their services to them. Post the article on your website or run it in your firm's digital or print publications and mailings. Conduct presentations using the PowerPoint that includes speaker notes. The flyer, which you may duplicate and distribute, is a good handout at presentations or can be mailed to clients.

SOC 1

(www.aicpa.org/interestareas/frc/assuranceadvisoryservices/pages/aicpasoc1report.aspx)

Article: Report on Controls at a Service Organization Relevant to User Entities' Internal Control over Financial Reporting

These reports, prepared in accordance with Statement on Standards for Attestation Engagements No. 16, *Reporting on Controls at a Service Organization*, are specifically intended to meet the needs of the managements of user entities and the user entities' auditors as they evaluate the effect of the controls at the service organization on the user entities' financial statement assertions. These reports are important components of user entities' evaluation of their internal controls over financial reporting for purposes of complying with laws and regulations, such as the Sarbanes-Oxley Act, and the user entities' auditors as they plan and perform audits of the user entities' financial statements. There are two types of reports for these engagements.

Comparison of SOC 1, SOC 2, and SOC 3 Reports

(www.aicpa.org/interestareas/frc/assuranceadvisoryservices/downloadabledocuments/comparisionofsoc1-3.doc)

Overview: The following chart provides a convenient, detailed comparison of SOC 1, SOC 2, and SOC 3 reports, including, but not limited to, the purpose and components of each of the three reports.

Table D-1: *Comparison of SOC 1, SOC 2, and SOC 3 Reports*

	SOC 1 Reports	SOC 2 Reports	SOC 3 Reports
Under what professional standard is the engagement performed?	SSAE No. 16, *Reporting on Controls at a Service Organization* AICPA Guide, *Applying SSAE No. 16, Reporting on Controls at a Service Organization*	AT 101, *Attestation Engagements* AICPA Guide, *Reporting on Controls at a Service Organization Relevant to Security, Availability, Processing Integrity, Confidentiality, or Privacy*	AT 101, *Attestation Engagements* AICPA Technical Practice Aid, *Trust Services Principles, Criteria, and Illustrations* (www.webtrust.net/downloads/WT.TrustServices.pdf)
What is the subject matter of the engagement?	Controls at a service organization relevant to user entities internal control over financial reporting.	Controls at a service organization relevant to security, availability, processing integrity confidentiality, or privacy. If the report addresses the privacy principle, the service organization's compliance with the commitments in its statement of privacy practices.	Controls at a service organization relevant to security, availability, processing integrity, confidentiality, or privacy. If the report addresses the privacy principle, the service organization's compliance with the commitments in its statement of privacy practices.
What is the purpose of the report?	To provide information to the auditor of a user entity's financial statements about controls at a service organization that may be relevant to a user entity's internal control over financial reporting. It enables the user auditor to perform risk assessment procedures, and if a type 2 report is provided, to assess the risk of material misstatement of financial statement assertions affected by the service organization's processing.	To provide management of a service organization, user entities, and other specified parties with information and a CPA's opinion about controls at the service organization that may affect user entities' security, availability, processing integrity, confidentiality or privacy. A type 2 report that addresses the privacy principle; also provides a CPA's opinion about the service organization's compliance with the commitments in its statement of privacy practices.	To provide interested parties with a CPA's opinion about controls at the service organization that may affect user entities' security, availability, processing integrity, confidentiality, or privacy. A report that addresses the privacy principle; also provides a CPA's opinion about the service organization's compliance with the commitments in its privacy notice.

(Continued)

Table D-1: *Comparison of SOC 1, SOC 2, and SOC 3 Reports (Continued)*

	SOC 1 Reports	SOC 2 Reports	SOC 3 Reports
What are the components of the report?	A description of the service organization's system. A service auditor's report that contains an opinion on the fairness of the presentation of the description of the service organization's system, the suitability of the design of the controls, and in a type 2 report, the operating effectiveness of the controls. In a type 2 report, a description of the service auditor's tests of the controls and the results of the tests.	A description of the service organization's system. A service auditor's report that contains an opinion on the fairness of the presentation of the description of the service organization's system, the suitability of the design of the controls, and in a type 2 report, the operating effectiveness of the controls. If the report addresses the privacy principle, the service auditor's opinion on whether the service organization complied with the commitments in its statement of privacy practices. In a type 2 report, a description of the service auditor's tests of controls and the results of the tests. In a type 2 report that addresses the privacy principle, a description of the service auditor's tests of the service organization's compliance with the commitments in its statement of privacy practices and the results of those tests.	A service auditor's report on whether the entity maintained effective controls over its system as it relates to the principle being reported on, that is, security, availability, processing integrity, confidentiality, or privacy, based on the applicable trust services criteria. If the report addresses the privacy principle, the service auditor's opinion on whether the service organization complied with the commitments in its statement of privacy practices.
Who are the intended users of the report?	Auditors of the user entity's financial statements, management of the user entities, and management of the service organization.	Parties that are knowledgeable about • the nature of the service provided by the service organization. • how the service organization's system interacts with user entities, subservice organizations, and other parties. • internal control and its limitations. • the criteria and how controls address those criteria.	Anyone.

AICPA SOC Products

***Service Organizations: Applying SSAE No. 16*, Reporting on Controls at a Service Organization Guide (SOC 1)**

(www.cpa2biz.com/AST/Main/CPA2BIZ_Primary/AuditAttest/IndustryspecificGuidance/PRDOVR~PC-0127910/PC-0127910.jsp)

This guide is designed to assist CPAs in transitioning from performing a service auditor's engagement under Statement on Auditing Standards (SAS) No. 70, *Service Organizations*, to doing so under Statement on Standards for Attestation Engagements No. 16, *Reporting on Controls at a Service Organization*, which replaces the guidance for service auditors in SAS No. 70.

Publications | eBook, Online Subscription, Paperback $60.00–$75.00

SERVICE ORGANIZATION CONTROL REPORTS SM: SOC 1, SOC 2, and SOC 3 On-Demand Series

(www.cpa2biz.com/AST/Main/CPA2BIZ_Primary/AuditAttest/PRDOVR~PC-780281/PC-780281.jsp)

This series of courses will provide information and guidance on the three new reporting options on controls at a service organization that have replaced SAS 70 reports.

CPE Self-Study | On-Demand $99.00–$236.25

***Reporting on Controls at a Service Organization Relevant to Security, Availability, Processing Integrity, Confidentiality, or Privacy* (SOC 2)**

(www.cpa2biz.com/AST/Main/CPA2BIZ_Primary/AuditAttest/Industryspecific Guidance/PRDOVR~PC-0128210/PC-0128210.jsp)

This new guide summarizes the three new SOC engagements and provides detailed guidance for performing examinations under AT section 101, *Attest Engagements* (AICPA, *Professional Standards*), to report on a service organization's controls over its system relevant to security, availability, processing integrity, confidentiality, or privacy, commonly referred to as a *SOC 2 engagement*.

Publications | eBook, Online Subscription, Paperback $60.00–$75.00

Service Organizations: New Reporting Options

(www.cpa2biz.com/AST/Main/CPA2BIZ_Primary/AuditAttest/Industryspecific Guidance/PRDOVR~PC-0224811/PC-0224811.jsp)

This alert provides information on a recently issued Statement on Standards for Attestation Engagements and a finalized Statement on Auditing Standards.

Publications | eBook, On-Demand, Online Subscription, Paperback $29.00–$53.75.

Appendix E

Reporting on Controls at a Cloud Computing Service Organization

This appendix describes cloud computing service organizations and provides an overview of the risks and challenges associated with performing a service organization controls (SOC) 2 engagement for cloud service organizations.[1]

A cloud computing service organization (cloud service organization) provides user entities with on-demand access to a shared pool of configurable computing resources (for example, networks, servers, storage, and applications). Cloud computing is becoming an important IT strategy for user entities that need varying levels of IT resources and for whom purchasing and maintaining sophisticated and costly IT resources is not an effective strategy.

[1] As we went to press, this document which is contained in appendix E of the May 1, 2011 SOC 2 Guide, *Reporting on Controls at a Service Organization Relevant to Security, Availability, Processing Integrity, Confidentiality or Privacy*, was in the process of being revised. Please check www.aicpa.org/interestareas/frc/assuranceadvisoryservices/pages/sorhome.aspx for the latest information contained in the June 2012 release of the SOC 2 Guide.

Definition of Cloud Computing

Although many definitions of the term *cloud computing* exist, the following definition from the National Institute of Standards and Technology (NIST)[2] is widely used:

Cloud computing is a model for enabling convenient, on-demand network access to a shared pool of configurable computing resources (e.g., networks, servers, storage, applications, and services) that can be rapidly provisioned and released with minimal management effort or service provider interaction. This cloud model promotes availability and is composed of five essential characteristics, three service models, and four deployment models.

Essential Characteristics:

- **On-demand self-service.** A consumer can unilaterally provision computing capabilities, such as server time and network storage, as needed automatically without requiring human interaction with each service's provider.
- **Broad network access.** Capabilities are available over the network and accessed through standard mechanisms that promote use by heterogeneous thin or thick client platforms (e.g., mobile phones, laptops, and PDAs).
- **Resource pooling.** The provider's computing resources are pooled to serve multiple consumers using a multi-tenant model, with different physical and virtual resources dynamically assigned and reassigned according to consumer demand. There is a sense of location independence in that the customer generally has no control or knowledge over the exact location of the provided resources but may be able to specify location at a higher level of abstraction (e.g., country, state, or datacenter). Examples of resources include storage, processing, memory, network bandwidth, and virtual machines.
- **Rapid elasticity.** Capabilities can be rapidly and elastically provisioned, in some cases automatically, to quickly scale out and rapidly released to quickly scale in. To the consumer, the capabilities available for provisioning often appear to be unlimited and can be purchased in any quantity at any time.
- **Measured service.** Cloud systems automatically control and optimize resource use by leveraging a metering capability at some level of abstraction appropriate to the type of service (e.g., storage, processing, bandwidth, and active user accounts). Resource usage can be monitored, controlled, and reported providing transparency for both the provider and consumer of the utilized service.

Service Models:

- **Cloud Software as a Service (SaaS).** The capability provided to the consumer is to use the provider's applications running on a cloud infrastructure. The applications are accessible from various client devices through a thin client interface such as a web browser (e.g., web-based email). The consumer does not manage or control the underlying cloud infrastructure including network, servers, operating systems, storage,

[2] Mell, Peter and Tim Grance, "The NIST Definition of Cloud Computing," Version 15 (October 7, 2009) http://csrc.nist.gov/groups/SNS/cloud-computing/.

or even individual application capabilities, with the possible exception of limited user specific application configuration settings.

- **Cloud Platform as a Service (PaaS).** The capability provided to the consumer is to deploy onto the cloud infrastructure consumer-created or acquired applications created using programming languages and tools supported by the provider. The consumer does not manage or control the underlying cloud infrastructure including network, servers, operating systems, or storage, but has control over the deployed applications and possibly application hosting environment configurations.
- **Cloud Infrastructure as a Service (IaaS).** The capability provided to the consumer is to provision processing, storage, networks, and other fundamental computing resources where the consumer is able to deploy and run arbitrary software, which can include operating systems and applications. The consumer does not manage or control the underlying cloud infrastructure but has control over operating systems, storage, deployed applications, and possibly limited control of select networking components (e.g., host firewalls).

Deployment Models:

- **Private cloud.** The cloud infrastructure is operated solely for an organization. It may be managed by the organization or a third party and may exist on premise or off premise.
- **Community cloud.** The cloud infrastructure is shared by several organizations and supports a specific community that has shared concerns (e.g., mission, security requirements, policy, and compliance considerations). It may be managed by the organizations or a third party and may exist on premise or off premise.
- **Public cloud.** The cloud infrastructure is made available to the general public or a large industry group and is owned by an organization selling cloud services.
- **Hybrid cloud.** The cloud infrastructure is a composition of two or more clouds (private, community, or public) that remain unique entities but are bound together by standardized or proprietary technology that enables data and application portability (e.g., cloud bursting for load-balancing between clouds).

Risks to User Entities

Although management of a user entity may outsource the IT functions to a cloud service organization, it cannot outsource its responsibility for the operations of those functions. As a result, management of a user entity may need to actively monitor and assess aspects of the cloud service organization's system that affect the services provided to the user entity. The very characteristics that make cloud computing an attractive solution may also increase certain risks to the user entities. For example:

- the increased sharing of system resources among user entities increases the risk that the activities of one user entity will adversely affect the availability, security, processing integrity, confidentiality, and privacy of the other user entities.

- the essential characteristics of cloud computing make it difficult to assess whether the cloud service organization is fulfilling certain commitments related to confidentiality and privacy that it has made to user entities, such as in contracts, service level agreements, or statements of privacy practices. For example, a cloud service organization may reallocate online data storage space between user entities to address the changing demands for resources. In these circumstances, the second user entity may be able to access the data of the original user of the storage space, unless the cloud service organization has controls to erase that data from the storage space.
- the aggregation of many user entities' data in a single cloud environment increases the attractiveness of the cloud computing organization as a target for attacks, given the extent of data that can potentially be compromised and misused.
- cloud providers spawn and retire virtual servers regularly to respond to changing user-entity demands. The transitory nature of these virtual servers increases the risk that unauthorized system changes are introduced in the respawning processes (bringing the server up again). In addition, this transitory nature increases the risk that traditional audit trails (for example, system logs or configuration reports) will not provide sufficient evidence of the functioning of controls for the cloud-based systems.
- the dynamic nature of cloud computing can result in the data being stored on different physical storage devices using different data security controls. As a result, data security controls designed with the assumption that data is stored in a static location may not be effective.

Challenges Faced by the Cloud Service Organization in Meeting Users' Information Needs

In order for management of a user entity to actively monitor and assess aspects of the cloud service organization's system that affect the services provided to the user entity, it will need information about the service organization's system. In providing such information, the cloud service organization faces many of the traditional challenges faced by service organizations, including the following:

- Controlling the cost and disruption resulting from inquiries and visits from multiple user entities who wish to obtain information about the system and test system controls that are relevant to those user entities. Adding to such costs and disruption is the time required to train user entity personnel about cloud services, processes, and architecture.
- Balancing the need to protect user entities' information against the need to provide governance, risk, and control information to existing and prospective user entities. For example, providing a user entity with detailed security configuration information regarding the cloud environment increases the risk that personnel at that user entity

will use that information to compromise security and gain access to other user entities' data.

- Balancing the need to provide information about the system to user entities in an effective and efficient manner against the need to protect the cloud service organization from risks, such as the disclosure of confidential user-entity information. For example, in a traditional data center setting, a user entity usually has access to all data and system resources for a dedicated e-mail server. If a cloud computing architecture comingles e-mails from multiple users in a single database, providing such access to all data and system resources in a cloud setting would compromise the confidentiality of other user entities' e-mail.

A service auditor's SOC 2 report can be an effective tool for communicating information about the cloud service organization's services and the suitability of the design and operating effectiveness of controls over the systems that provides these services. It can provide assurance to existing and prospective user entities regarding the service organization's services, including confidence in the security, availability, and processing integrity of the system and controls over data confidentiality and privacy of information. This additional confidence can help the cloud service organization address the concerns of prospective and existing customers in a consistent and comprehensive manner, rather than having to customize a response to specific requirements of different user entities. In a new and developing industry, such confidence can help increase the rate of adoption of a cloud service organization's services and the extent to which user entities are willing to trust critical operations to the cloud environment.

Risk Considerations When Performing a SOC 2 Engagement for a Cloud Service Organization

Performing a SOC 2 engagement for a cloud service organization is conceptually the same as performing such an engagement for any other service organization that provides IT services. However, when performing these engagements, the service auditor needs to pay particular attention to matters such as the following:

- **Shared responsibility.** The responsibility for controls is shared between the user entities and service organization. One challenge of providing cloud services is that different user entities will often require varying levels of service and related responsibility and accountability on the part of the cloud service organization. In these situations, the service auditor needs to consider the processes and controls that the cloud service organization has in place to address the differing requirements of its user entities.
- **Information life cycle management when reporting on confidentiality and privacy.** Information life cycle management is one of the most challenging aspects of managing a cloud, particularly when addressing privacy requirements. Because cloud service organizations have multiple clients sharing system resources, and these

shared resources (for example, servers and storage devices) may be reallocated among the clients depending on needs at a given time, information life cycle management for any particular client may become highly complex and challenging to administer.

- **Comingling of data when reporting on confidentiality and privacy.** Many SaaS environments comingle the data of user entities in a single database. As a result, it may be difficult to completely destroy or return user entity data at the end of its life cycle or at the end of the relationship between a user entity and cloud service provider.
- **Transnational data processing and storage.** Many types of data, including personal information, are subject to specific laws and regulations in the jurisdiction in which the data is created or in which the data subject is a resident of, including restrictions on the transfer of data to other jurisdictions. Cloud service providers may be unaware of the particular requirements for any one user entity, and the multinational architecture of a cloud infrastructure may result in unintended violations of laws and regulations by the user entity.
- **Availability, continuity of operations, and disaster recovery when reporting on availability.** Cloud computing environments are inherently complex due to the need to support multiple clients with varying system requirements (for example, different operating systems and virtual servers) and variations in the demand for resources among clients. Due to this complexity, techniques for maintaining system availability, providing for continuity of operations when a disruption has occurred, and recovering from a disaster vary significantly from traditional techniques. The flexibility provided by cloud architecture usually provides the cloud with the technological ability to recover user entity processing on different hardware operating in the same or a different facility but requires more complex processes and controls to do so.
- **Virtualization technologies.** Although not unique to a cloud, the implementation, configuration, protection, operation, and support of virtualization hypervisors is critical to most cloud computing environments. A *hypervisor* is a software program that manages multiple operating systems on a single computer system. Hypervisors need to be configured and managed to meet the combined security, availability, and processing integrity needs of customers. A service auditor needs to understand the hypervisor(s) used by the cloud service organization and the unique policies, procedures, and processes used to configure and maintain them. The service auditor also needs to address the same issues with regard to any applications or software infrastructure provided in a multitenancy environment.
- **Transitory nature of virtual environments.** Because of the virtual nature of individual user-entity processing environments and the highly dynamic nature of resource allocation, traditional testing strategies related to system configuration may not provide sufficient evidence about the operating effectiveness of controls. Similarly, audit evidence traditionally used to evaluate the operation of the control may not exist or may not be sufficiently reliable when testing in a cloud environment. The service auditor needs to give consideration to these factors in planning and performing his or her examination.

- **Encryption and key management.**[3] Encryption is generally an effective way of protecting information in a cloud computing environment. Encryption of data may be the responsibility of the user entity, cloud service organization, or both and may vary from user entity to user entity within any one cloud computing environment. A cloud service organization needs to have processes and controls in place to meet its responsibilities, in accordance with service level agreements. In addition, processes and controls are needed to protect encryption keys during key generation, storage, use, change, and destruction.

Engagement Acceptance Considerations for the Service Auditor

Prior to accepting an engagement to report on controls at a service organization related to the trust services principles, a practitioner should consider whether he or she has the necessary skills and knowledge to perform the examination or will need to use the work of a specialist with the necessary skills and knowledge.

In performing a SOC 2 engagement for a cloud service organization, a service auditor needs to consider the following:

- Whether the cloud environment is private, public, community, or hybrid and the different risks that each deployment model brings to the environment.
- Whether the description is sufficient to meet the needs of user entities based on industry and regulatory considerations. The cloud service provider's description of its system should address unique aspects that cloud computing brings to common processes, including the following:
  - Data governance
  - Information leakage
  - Hardware disposal
  - Hypervisor security and change control
  - Spawning and retirement of virtual systems
  - Encryption
  - Incident management
  - Use of third parties

  Because of the rapidly evolving nature of cloud computing, service auditors should consider consulting the publications and online resources of organizations that address cloud computing, including the NIST, the European Network and Information Security Agency, and the Cloud Security Alliance (CSA).

[3] *Encryption* is a form of security that turns information, images, programs, or other data into unreadable cipher by applying a set of complex algorithms to the original material. These algorithms transfer the data into streams or blocks of seemingly random alphanumeric characters. An encryption key might encrypt, decrypt, or perform both functions, depending on the type of encryption software being used.

- When reporting on privacy in a cloud environment, how privacy risks are affected by the shared aspects of a cloud environment, including the following:
  - Privacy policies and notices
  - Breach notice
  - Access
  - Regulatory requirements
  - The types of personal information in the cloud environment and its sensitivity
  - Sharing of information with third parties
- Whether the controls identified are sufficiently responsive to the applicable trust services criteria, given the dynamic nature of cloud computing and the particular risks associated with it.
- Whether the results of tests of controls will be sufficient to support the auditor's opinion, given the dynamic nature of infrastructure considerations. For example, security configurations of hypervisors and servers are subject to frequent modification throughout the period. Tests that infer the operating effectiveness of controls through inspection of the results of their operation (for example, inspection of security configuration files) are likely to be less effective, unless performed throughout the report period using a statistical-based sampling approach.

Cloud Security Frameworks

Due to the immaturity and rapid growth of cloud computing, cloud service organizations and their user entities are still refining the security processes and controls that should be in place at the service organization. To aid in this effort, cloud service organizations and user entities have joined together with governmental bodies in several different efforts to develop frameworks for assessing risks, processes, and controls for a cloud environment. Implementation of a framework could be demonstrated by a SOC 2 report in which the description of the system includes descriptions of the framework used, the processes designed to address the framework requirements, and controls implemented in response to the framework requirements.

One leading framework has been developed by the CSA. This framework consists of the following:

- Consensus assessment questions that have been developed to help user entities gather information relevant to the security and availability of a cloud service provider's system
- Common controls matrix that provides cloud service providers and user entities with illustrative controls

More information on the CSA framework can be found at https://cloudsecurityalliance.org/.